Noise From The Rulers Of Darkness

Eximer Carriere

"*For we wrestle not against flesh and blood, but against principalities, against powers, against the rulers of the darkness of this world, against spiritual wickedness in high places".*

Ephesians 6:12

Copyright Information and Permissions

Copyright © 2013 CowCatLily Publishing

All rights reserved. No part of this book may be reproduced in any form or by any electronic or mechanical means, including information storage and retrieval systems, without written permission from the author and CowCatLily Publishing.

Any trademarks, service marks, product names or names featured are assumed to be the property of the respective owners and are used only for reference.

There is no implied endorsement if we use one of these terms.

Published by CowCatLily Publishing. Distributed in Canada by CowCatLily Publishing.

All audio recordings and images, including front cover design and photo, are registered trademarks of CowCatLily Publishing 2013. All rights reserved. June 2013

Any duplication prohibited without express written permission.

Scripture references are from the King James Version of the Bible.

The names of some people places and things have been changed to protect identities.

Copyright © 2013 All rights reserved.

ISBN: 0-9876956

ISBN-13: 978-0-9876956-2-8

CONTENTS

Dedication

Acknowledgements

Introduction

Preface

Chapter One; We've Only Just Begun	Pg # 1
Chapter Two; Is This True?	Pg #13
Chapter Three; Are You Talking To Me?	Pg #29
Chapter Four; This Could Be War	Pg #43
Chapter Five; I Will Survive	Pg #71
Chapter Six; We Have More Tricks	Pg #95
Chapter Seven; We Lived In Heaven	Pg #119
Chapter Eight; It's You We Hate	Pg #139
Chapter Nine; Running Out Of Time	Pg #155
Chapter Ten; Hi, I Want A Friend	Pg #169
Chapter Eleven; This Ain't Like Heaven	Pg #193
Chapter Twelve; The Darkness Fell	Pg #203
Chapter Thirteen; The Things In Between	Pg #215
Chapter Fourteen; The Things That I've Seen	Pg #227
About The Author	Pg #235

Dedication

To Jesus Christ, and all demon warriors.

Deuteronomy 18: 10 -12   [10]***There shall not be found among you.... a consulter with familiar spirits...*** [12]*For all that do these things are an abomination unto the **LORD**: ....*

{Bold and Italic added}

The objective of this book is to make people aware of the dangers of ghost hunting and just how real the spirit world is.

Acknowledgements

We would like to acknowledge the following people who were involved in making this book possible. Thank you for the hard work and effort ensuring that integrity was used in fulfilling the completion of this work.

Written and edited by Eximer Carriere

Book cover design, editing and marketing director, Cristina Carriere

Proof reading, Laura Ovenden

A special thanks to my dear wife and best friend Cristina who supported me through all the insanity of experiencing the haunting and subsequent oppression from it all. Without her true love for me I don't know where I'd be and I am truly blessed. Ilario and Mary raised a great daughter.

Also my heartfelt gratitude to Chris T. and Pastor John C. for their care, friendship and solid help through my darkest hours.

My appreciation goes out to Laura Ovenden for her friendship and her humble desire to help direct the progress of this book so I could write it to the best of my ability.

A special thank you to my dear mother Bernadette for trying to teach me right from wrong throughout my life, and her undying faith in God and her strong disposition. The Lord has provided me with some of my faith and determination because of her life's example. She is one of the strongest people that I know.

Lastly I should thank the ghosts and demons that inhabit the air ways, for without them this audio book wouldn't exist. I am grateful for the opportunity to expose them for the evil entities that they are.

All glory is given to Almighty God who is my chosen Lord and the Saviour of this fallen world. Without Him, I wouldn't be breathing.

Preface

Writing this audio book was a labor of love.

I found it important to not only document what really happened, but to make available the audio portion as well, to prove without doubt just how real the concept of invisible entities that are a part of life the way we know it, truly are.

I believe that we as people, when we hear the truth about something in life, we know it in our hearts. We just do. Any kind of truth sets people free, but there is only so much truth out there, and the rest are outright lies or are mixed with truth which in turn make them unreliable.

It is vitally important to be as honest as we can be in life. There seems to be no contentment to our existence if we don't acknowledge reality whether good or bad and I believe some of the bad is due to making bad choices, like rejecting Gods truths and blatantly or ignorantly discarding them. Our lives are filled with blessings and curses.

I'm not a fanatic, nor do I think I know much compared to many people, but I know what I've lived. We all do.

The following story might draw you in and hopefully help you to believe that the devil and his demons exist, our enemies whether we realize it or not.

Knowledge of an enemy is important in any battle. We can access Gods supernatural strength, wisdom and love. All we need is a sincere heart and faith in Jesus Christ, and in knowing He can deliver us from whatever we are dealing with if we ask for his help and guidance, and act on it.

The bible also says that there is pleasure in sin for a season. But then comes death, physical or spiritual. Everything is in Gods hands. He loves us unconditionally but also chastises those who believe in him, because he cares.

I was disciplined from the motel nightmare. I was also loved. It was terrifying and difficult. God spared me this time.

Chapter One; We've Only Just Begun

2nd Timothy 2: 26 **And that they may recover themselves out of the snare of the devil, who are taken captive by him at his will.**

This is a true story. That fact I needed to keep reminding myself of as I wrote these words with what seemed like insanity, with all the unbelievable incidents at the Park Sets Motel. This is a story with twists and turns about the spirit world mixing in with us humans.

This audio book is about encounters with ghosts. It is hopefully going to entertain you as well as I hope open your eyes, ears and spirit to haunting encounters with rulers of the darkness. If you have ever experienced spiritual attacks you will relate to this reality. Maybe we're not mad after all. I know I'm not, but the ghosts and demons I associated with each day surely were. I've tried to describe the feelings and sometimes fear of going to work each day in the knowledge that the building was haunted and how to get through the day and not get the hell scared out of me.

I'm still amazed when I think of all the lunacy that the spirits put me and my co workers through. As I write these words I feel forever grateful to Almighty God. I believe if He leads me to it He'll lead me through it. I believe He allowed me to fight the battles and protected my sorry soul all the way through the ordeal.

I was dealing with ghosts and they are quite evil and tricky and they seem to enjoy scaring and confusing people.

They think they are brave and they think they are smart, and some of them are. I can scarcely believe the amount of activity I experienced in and around the concrete giant nick named the dark tower. All the voices from the other side of hell with some good still photo pics of my ghastly foes. I don't recommend taunting the spirit world but that's how I handled my fear of them. That might be why I did it just to feel more in control, as a person should be when dealing with things like this. It can be a matter of personal safety. I have learned that spirits can and do hurt people. There aren't many guarantees when you decide to battle back at resentful angry spirits.

I have pieced together the stories of the hauntings that sometimes seemed so scrambled. The ghosts that haunted the motel were not impressed with us working there. They more or less tolerated people being around them. I had the privilege of meeting, however brief in the months I was working there the long term maintenance man who told me he had worked at the tower since 1978. His name was Carey and he was nice and all but he kind of creeped us out. He was too quiet and aloof, the kind of person who could pass for a ghost. You wouldn't notice him until he was around the corner. The stories he told me about suicides and other occurrences will be mentioned in this book. Suffice it to say Carey had informed me one day that there were 'lots of ghosts here, hundreds'.

My first day at work at the tower was like any new job. It was early in February, and it was a nice mild day as my alarm went off at four thirty in the morning. I had planned to be up early enough to start psyching myself out to face the new environment of people and work.

I got lost looking for the place but I eventually found it. A tall motel at 26 storeys, a concrete monstrosity with windows working their way around the perfect shape of a parallelogram, like a six sided fortress. I wondered what kind of work I would be doing and told myself I would take it one day at a time. I enjoyed my last sip of coffee not knowing how much I would look forward to getting out of that tower to enjoy one, sometimes driving back and plotting my next strategic move as to how to outsmart the malevolent spirits in that sad oppressive building.

I met the boss named Lucas and waited inside the long hallway entrance to the tower along with a couple of other men.

There were seven workers at first; Rudy, Matt, Papa, Dario, Dace, Roy and me. A week after starting we received a few days pay which is when we all met the owner of the renovation company, Hector. Lucas was Hectors son.

The first of the workers I met was an African guy named Haemin, or as he would prefer us to call him, his nick name; Rudy. He could usually be found on the main floor, texting his girlfriends. Rudy and I worked together the first few weeks pushing wheelbarrows full of blocks and dust from the elevators, down the main hallway entrance and outside to a Bobcat™ machine where the driver would move it to the different bins.

Another guy named Matt was from Ecuador. He was the kind of person you couldn't help but like. He was charismatic and comical. A few times he showed up at work looking pretty rough, sometimes worried about how he would pay back the gamblers he dealt with. At first Matt showed up for each work day but eventually started skipping days. Someone in our crew eventually gave him the nickname of 'Skipper'. I could tell this was going to be a fun environment.

Silvio was our foreman and a real good guy. Blessings to him for helping me out of some tense situations during my time working at the Park Sets Motel. Silvio was from Brazil and amused us at times with his various martial arts stances. He used to make us laugh every chance he could and at least once first thing in the morning. Silvio had the daunting tasks of everything involved with supervising the gutting of the motel. Supervising was more like babysitting a sleeping giant.

He would usually show up around 6:45 a.m. and let us in through the back at the service doors in front of the short driveway. We would go through the back of the building and take a few short hallways around to the three passenger elevators and take one of the two that were working up to the 3rd floor.

Papa was another worker in the crew. Papa weighed in at probably 280lbs., was a short quiet man with a gentle disposition and he was always wearing a small colorful cap. He was born in Africa. He was a gentle giant but most people would not have wanted to upset him. He was a humble person and physically powerful.

Dario was another worker sent to the motel. He was friendly and easy going. He was Portuguese. He was a good worker and fun to be around and that's something we all seemed to do was try to have a good day and everybody get along. It helped in getting through each day just a little easier.

One of the workers that stands out to me during my stay there was Dace. Dace was 37 years old from Jamaica and extremely funny. He would talk with a sharp accent and say something funny cracking us all up, someone to help keep a good mood going in a hard work environment. Dace was as strong as an ox. He was about six feet tall a lanky guy but tough and resourceful. He had his favorite shovel. The shovel he always used was three and half feet long with a wooden handle and a small steel scoop for shoveling. It was humorous to see him use such a small shovel, but he still did more work than the rest of us. The shovel was his trademark. He had to have it. I looked forward to working with him and we got a lot of work done in those six trying months.

The Bobcat™ driver on the site was named Roy. He was also from Jamaica and an interesting, intelligent person. He was a tall guy with a slow and deliberate pace to his walk. He would speak his mind and tell you how he thought things really were and many times he was right. Roy and I had something in common. We both faced obstacles head on if we had to. That mind-set came in handy working in that spooky place.

The motel was once a beautiful five star rated luxury motel well known of at the time and now being turned into a residential setting. I sometimes felt guilty, almost uneasy for being a part of the renovations, bashing out walls of the motels recent grandiose condition. Something was making me feel like I shouldn't be demolishing anything though I was grateful for the opportunity to work in the interesting building.

It always had an intimidating feeling about it though. The air always felt heavy. Though most of the electricity had been disabled so the motel could be renovated it felt like you were being watched or a sudden gush of cool air would be noticed. There were a number of times when I would walk the hallway I could swear something had touched my ear.

There were temporary railings on the 24th floor which was the only floor that was partially open to the floor beneath, replacing the two motel rooms in front of the three passenger elevators. The opening was once graced with an elaborate railing wrapping around the spiral staircase down to the 23rd floor which provided a common sitting area with a spectacular view of the city's downtown skyline. The two storey window view was relaxing after a good meal at one of the four restaurants adjoining the tower. A nice way to unwind before a restful sleep in your luxurious room in the motel.

Cinder block walls wound their way around each floor connecting the hall sections to the different rooms. Most of the floors had twelve rooms, each with a scenic view. All the rooms were identical except for the two rooms facing the front elevators which had a door that could be unlocked to make it a double suite. There were three main passenger elevators for the guests and visitors and two service elevators for staff and service personnel. The #1 elevator was tarped off and out of service. It would never work.

As February finally ended and March rolled in, all thoughts for me turned to spring. That happy optimistic time when days are getting longer and weather is warming up. I was enthusiastic coming into work, everyone gathering in our makeshift tool room, old motel room 353, talking about life in general while getting ready for another back breaking day of work to forever change the interior history of the once fabulous motel.

The front of the motel faces east so the sun would be bright and warm in the morning then slowly creep around to the back service elevator area where it was always cool in temperature and actually almost too cool even on a sizzling hot day.

The building's tower was constructed with windows going all the way around, forming the shape of the parallelogram. I remember early on especially after each floor had been renovated and the snow outside had melted, just how beautiful the view was from just about anywhere in the tower and the higher the floor the more scenic the sight was, being able to see city skylines with all the buildings surrounding the area, concrete structures that looked so impressive.

Every room had to more or less be dismantled, butchered to its core. For about a month some of us would pick a room and take down everything in it. After a few weeks my body had become used to all the physical abuse I was putting it through although I was dead tired.

There were plenty of ways to get hurt or worse, especially from falls through exposed holes until they were securely covered. Getting cut and badly scratched was also a common occurrence from all the sharp wires that made up the inner shell of the plastered walls.

As I got used to the daily routine I noticed my breathing was more and more obstructed. There were only small pieces of asbestos around us but there were still plenty of other contaminates as well. I remember noticing black soot at different places and in varying degrees on some of the walls and ceilings in the tower.

I started investigating the different floors, at first sneaking away during break times. As I walked around I noticed all the different views around the building as far as my eye could see. I went to the top floor and explored the great view. The 25th floor was considered a private floor which at one time had been the floor where the former motel's employees had worked. I noticed the outlines of what used to be the block walls dividing the different offices and the lunch room and water cooler. Each office had a sliding balcony door that lead out to some privacy because of the concrete slabs on each side.

As we started our Monday morning everyone was in their usual sluggish rhythm. We were working on the 16th floor and were just about finished. Silvio started moving us around and leaving two of us behind to finish up the odds and ends. As I would find out there was always a lot of finish work and as time went by more and more was added on.

'Morning Dace, how are you man?'

'Hey hey, hey, Exi, Exi morning brother not bad, not bad but tired as hell Exi, bumba clad man this place is killing me; tap tap tap tap tap all day tell ya man enough to wear you out and make you feel crazy know what I mean?'

Dace would have drywall work lined up and work until about midnight or so, then come in to the motel the next day. I don't know how he did it as he was really tired but still got more done most times than anyone else. I had respect for Dace. We worked well together and had a lot of laughs.

In March the pace at work picked up as we had dreaded. As the pace quickened the elevator work was doubled and Silvio had me and Matt do most of it. I earned my pay as we all did. So for a few days in the week I was slugging it out and the other days doing the elevator job. It was nostalgic being in the old elevators too. Silvio had warned us not to operate the control buttons in the elevators unless we were assigned to them. They were unpredictable and you couldn't flick the service buttons too quickly or you would get stuck inside it either opened or closed. I made certain I was careful with the buttons as I got used to operating elevators #2 and #3.

I was trying to check out the upper floors and the tower in general to get some pictures and videos of the beautiful tower or at least what was left of its elegance. On a Thursday I got my chance to take some pictures from inside.

During the morning break I went to my truck to get a sandwich then headed up early so I could obtain some video footage. I was excited to take them and be able to show my wife Tina the inside of the building. I headed down the hall to the elevators. Elevator #3 opened its carpet laden self up and waited patiently for me to push the buttons. I leaned up against the carpet draped across the back of the box to protect the full length mirror that inter joined the wood veneer in its once regal condition. The doors opened and I walked out and entered room 2445. I turned on the camera and switched to video mode to start filming the view. The sun was hiding behind the clouds but it was still bright outside. I narrated.

'This is the view from work, quite beautiful.'

As I walked out of the room I turned left and passed the temporary rail that blocked off the opening to the once spiral staircase then walked past the purple striped stairwell into room 2449. The two stairwells are located a short distance from both corners of the foyer where the passenger elevators are, down the hallways in either direction to the motel rooms.

One stairwell has a purple stripe running diagonally all the way down the building. The other has a grey stripe.

As I went back down to my truck I felt a sense of accomplishment in getting some pictures of the great old motel. I'd wanted to do it for a while but I kept putting it off until I was more familiar with the design of the motel. It was maze like.

After arriving home I went through my routine. I looked forward to the refreshing taste of a cold beverage and relaxing until Tina was home from work. Relaxing seemed like a reward for working so hard, with a cold drink soothing my throat and washing down any remaining dust. The weekend was here, and Saturday was my day to sleep in and I always looked forward to the much needed rest.

That evening I remembered the video I had taken and asked Tina to help me download it. I had shot four short separate videos. While watching the second one I noticed something white moving across the screen.

'Tina, what the hell is that?'

'What is what?' she asked.

'There, check it out'.

I paused the video and rewound to where I saw a patchy white blob. As we watched and re watched the video we both had our developing opinions as to what it was we were looking at.

'Tina I can't believe it but to me that looks like some dude wearing a white dinner jacket.'

I had to scurry off the chair as this was just too unnerving.

'Brr, brr', I said out loud as a long shiver ran down my whole body. I'll never forget that sensation.

'That's just crazy Exi. I think that looks like his head. I've never seen anything like that before.'

'I just realized, that's where I work. Do you think that's a ghost?'

'Oh no doubt. What else could that be?'

'What am I gonna do Tina I can't tell the guys at work they'll think I'm losing my mind. Some of them might not appreciate me telling them the motel is haunted. I've got to watch that again there's no way. There's gotta be an explanation for it.'

I played it over and over again then checked the other videos if I could see anything else but that was all I saw. The white suit shaped image that did look like a man in a dinner jacket with black pants. His arm also seemed to move and I noticed he had a head with a face and eyes. I just couldn't believe it. I spent an hour or so going through the videos. Then I hoped I had an answer for the white figure. I remembered each floor had two fire hose extinguisher cabinets located to the left of each of the two exit doors leading to the stairwells.

'I'll bet you that's a fire hose Tina; that's all I can think of and that must be that white shape because the hose is white. First chance I get I need to debunk this, I have to it would be way too bizarre if that was a ghost.'

'Yeah but Exi that sure looks like a man to me you can see his head and everything.'

As Tina and I talked about the white object, I wondered whether I could find any information about the Park Sets Motel's past. I connected to the internet and started searching for anything I could find. It was difficult getting much about the motel on line. Most newspaper article archives didn't go back to the seventies or eighties. But what I found seemed to help put some of the pieces of this new real life puzzle more into perspective. I managed to find a handful of articles from a local newspaper and a couple of more from America. What I found shook my spirit.

'Nine die in inferno'. 'Killer fire's cause unknown.' 'Human error tops the fire's causes.'

As I read as much as I could about the tragic fire that happened back in 1978, I felt disheartened and numb like it was all a dream. As the minutes turned into hours I was alone as Tina had gone to bed; alone with my thoughts and overwhelmed as to how I felt and how things could play out at work. I felt the need to tell someone but who? I struggled with an uneasy feeling about working in the tower. Did I really film a ghost? My thoughts changed from fear to confusion as I struggled with how I was going to let at least some of the people at work know that there had been a fire and people had died.

Time had passed quickly and it was almost three a.m. I had to be up in three hours to face my new reality. I drifted off to sleep not feeling like myself anymore, like something inside me had changed. I felt a little discouraged as if an enemy had invaded my life, almost like I had to watch my back and be ready for anything.

'There's no way' I thought, chuckling as I tried to sleep; 'that's a white fire hose not a ghost. Life's just not like that everything is okay'.

I would end up eating those words. My life would never be the same and everything would not be okay.

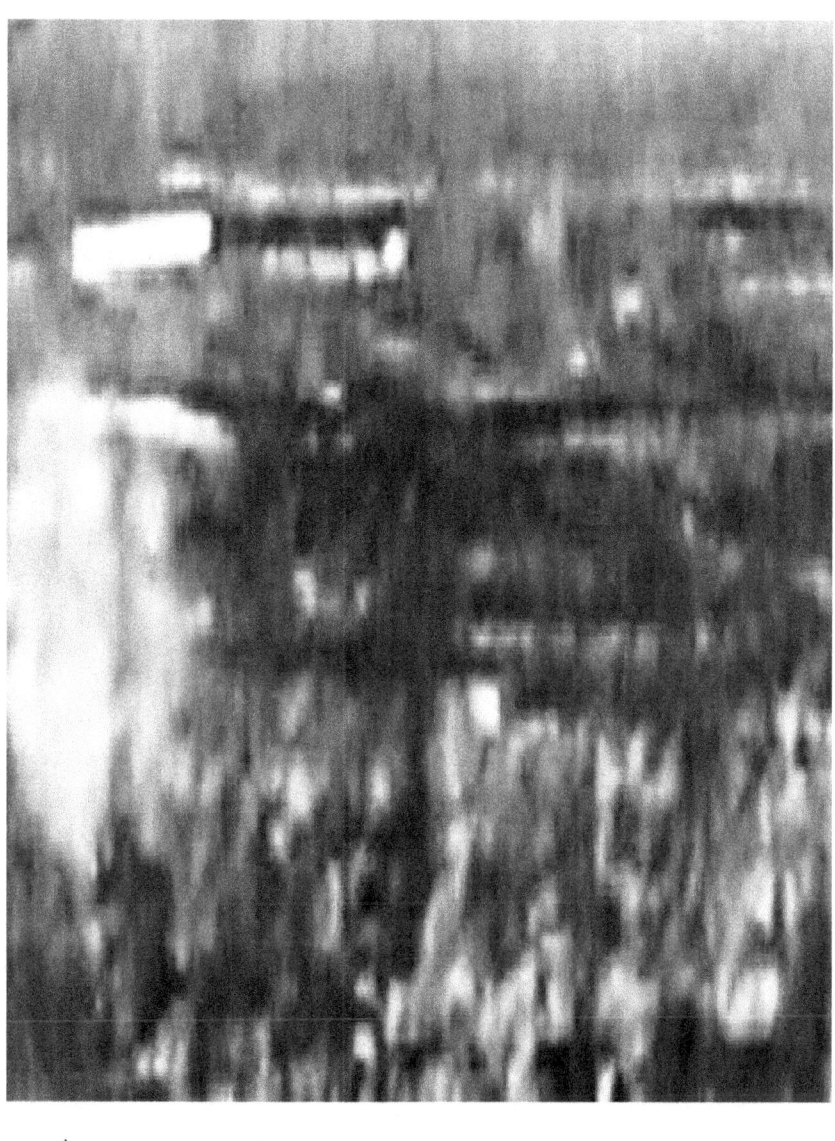

↑

The white blob I noticed while taking a digital video early on. I called him jackson.

Chapter Two; Is This True?

2nd Timothy 1: 7 **For God hath not given us the spirit of fear; but of power, and of love, and of a sound mind.**

Oh brother was I tired, stumbling around to wake up from a restless sleep. I managed to spill some coffee as I went out onto the balcony to have a smoke and take in the view from the 7th floor. As the coffee sort of kicked in I thought of the information I had found about the Park Sets Motel with the devastating deadly fire more than thirty years ago. My thoughts were scattered about telling anyone else about these findings. I finally decided I would print out the info and let Silvio our foreman know about the fire that occurred on January19th, 1978.

Rushing around, I managed to leave on time and joined the thousands of commuters on the expressways to get to the motel. As I arrived at work I reminded myself of the printed papers and put them under my shirt. The usual group of workers were there as we waited for Silvio to arrive in his little blue Hyundai™.

'Morning, morning,' he said as he stumbled with his key to unlock the pad lock.

We all seemed tired as we shuffled into the elevator to the third floor. Everyone was quiet as we changed and got ready for the day.

I walked down the hallway to the tool room and gathered up tools that I would need. I rolled one of the wheelbarrows down the hallway and around to the elevators. I walked around the 3rd floor taking time to look at the walls. There was still wallpaper hanging here and there. The crown moldings and baseboards were still their pearl white color and some rooms still had the flowered carpet, popular décor at the time that hadn't been disposed of yet. This floor would be the last one to demolish as we worked our way down the tower.

Walking around the floor I noticed Silvio.

'Hey Silvio, can I talk to you when you have a minute?'

'Everything okay?'

'Oh yeah buddy just want to ask you something.'

'Yeah no problem Exi, give me a minute'.

While waiting I pulled the papers from under my shirt.

'Yes you wanted to ask me something?'

'Morning Silvio, no not really can I talk to you in private'?

We walked to the office room as I started telling him how last night I looked up the history of the tower on line;

'I didn't find much, but I printed them out for you. I hope you don't mind Silvio cause its pretty tragic and sad, creepy too. I don't want to be the only one to know about this. I knew I could trust you. I didn't want to freak any of the other guys out. I don't know if you even want to read it, it's up to you I just needed you to know. People died in here that's all I'll tell you for now my friend, creeps me out Silvio'.

As I patted his shoulder I tried to smile but it didn't seem to work. I left him there with his thoughts as he stared into space and hoped that he would check out the information about this monstrosity of a building with such a gloomy past.

I boarded the elevator with Roy and Rudy; they headed downstairs to get ready to do their work for the day. The elevator doors opened and Dario stepped in, out of breath. 'Hey Exi, how are you?'

'Pretty good, and you Dario?'

'Not bad, rushing around, did you see Silvio, was he looking for me?'

'No, don't worry about it, you're right on time'.

He pressed the button for the third floor.

I went up to a higher floor that I was on the day before.

As I shoveled the cinder blocks that morning my thoughts were on proving that the white figure I had filmed was in fact a fire hose wrapped up in one of the cabinets inset on a wall. I was almost certain that there wasn't a spirit hanging out up there, that it didn't exist. Even though those people had died a tragic death in the past fire, and I would imagine a motel this big and old would have accumulated its share of suicides, it couldn't be haunted. I considered myself a rational person as I try to reason things through. I don't mind a good mystery. I knew I needed to go back up to the 24th floor and take more video to re trace my steps and see if I could zoom in to what had to be the fire hose. There was nothing else up there that was white.

About an hour had gone by when I noticed Silvio walking towards me. He motioned for Matt to come over. Matt was wondering what was up as Silvio told him about the nine people dying in the fire. He asked Matt not to tell the guys about the motels past because he knew they could be superstitious at times. He didn't want anyone quitting over it so we were supposed to keep it quiet. He had only told Matt and Dario. I remember by the end of the day we were all talking about it. I didn't feel comfortable telling any of them I was getting images on video so I kept that part to myself. A few of us were excited and spooked. Some of the others were pretty quiet. Matt was making fun of it all while Dario, Silvio and I took it in stride.

What are you going to do? People die all the time. It was a weird feeling to be renovating a building where people had died though. We accepted it and tried to ignore any negative thoughts.

March was very mild that year. Though the birds were chirping and that familiar spring feeling was all around, inside the motel it was cold. I had to remember this was a huge concrete shell with no heat, and only minimum electricity. It took a while for it to warm up in there but the back elevator areas were always cold. I guess it was because they were in the centre or the core of the tower.

Waking up for work the next day I had decided to get more video of the Park Sets Motel. While arriving at work I turned the video camera on to film the large building. The looming tower was on my right as I climbed the hill onto Emery Avenue and it definitely looked a bit run down and sad but majestic as it sat on its perch on the corner of the two streets that met in a T.

Winding my way right onto Jessup Street, I climbed up and turned into the driveway that leads up to the four newer built condos. On the left is the Park Sets Motel main lobby which is open for business. The 2nd floor hallway takes you to the different shops and the ballrooms, which were empty and locked while the work went on. The passenger elevators are down a second hallway at the centre of the tower. The lobby hallway is joined to the tower. Further up the driveway is an auto repair shop, the service bay built near the first motel that was demolished, and the former outdoor pool was now just a dumping ground for all the unwanted memories from its much taller sibling.

I parked in one of my favorite spots and went through the ritual of most mornings by sipping on coffee psyching myself out for the adventure of the work day that always lay ahead. Rudy had to take a day off so today I did his regular job of wheeling the barrows full from the front entrance of the elevators down the hallway and outside for Roy, then bring them back for Matt who would take them up the elevators to the work floor. It gave me an opportunity to take a video of all the furniture that was being stored from the former motel rooms in the Parks Sets Motel. The stuff was locked up in the old kids play area rooms and in the indoor pool area on the main floor. The door faces the elevators. It's a room with glass walls that form the hallways so I could see all the old antiques, tables, chairs, carpets, five foot long ottomans, lamps with full shades, fancy mirrors and the pictures that used to adorn the expensive papered walls.

There it all was. I wanted some of these artifacts but they were being thrown out as far as any of us knew. If that was true it was a shame.

March was rolling into April and I hadn't made it up to the floor yet. I hadn't had much chance lately as all of us were working together.

I managed to get some video of the 11th floor piles of rubble and with some of the rooms still intact displaying the room and how it was set up, peering into a wall less lavish bathroom with a corded telephone hanging on the wall conveniently mounted beside the toilet.

There was a totally different look on the second floor. The elevators opened up to grand double storied glass windows that allowed all of the mid day's sunshine in. It split apart into two hallways; left took you to the main lobby, to the left and down in the basement was one of the first discotheques in Ontario called 'Le Place'. It also took you to the Brass, Willow, and Haven rooms. There was also the 'Tiny' Lounge and a few boutiques, the conference rooms, the Terrain room and the infamous Continental Ballroom. Going right brought you out to more conference rooms, the Jasmine Ballroom, entrance to the outdoor pool, some of the suites and the Silver Lounge.

The wallpaper must have cost a fortune in those days. It was a pattern of vertical inch wide pale white stripes on a faint pastel green color, just beautiful. The floors were made of marble with a polished finish. Large windows draped down the long hallway with the rich, dark brown trim and baseboards and looked very elegant. This part of the motel looked like it was staying pretty much untouched. I remember that made me feel better for the tower's past. Something was actually staying intact.

The land mark motel that once stood across from this majestic main hallway was gone forever. The roof that was constructed to look like The Milky Way from the sky, nothing but its memory was left. A shame really. The late architect who had designed it for a friend must have rolled over in his grave.

Sometimes on the way up in the elevator, I would stop it at the second floor so I could remember what the other floors used to look like.

Not long after we had learned about the deaths from the fire some weird things started happening. There was no set pattern but odd things that kept happening; well they were hard to explain. For example a number of the guys used to use the back washrooms on the main floor beside the men's change room leading to the indoor pool. One day Matt was down there alone washing the dust off from the days work in one of the sinks. As he washed up he said the water from the sink furthest away from him started running on its own. He hurried out of there it scared him so much.

At quitting time Silvio was alone checking the windows and doors and as he would walk around each floor making his way down the motel he would feel his ears were getting flicked. He said it usually happened in front of the two stairwells and on many occasions. He said it scared him and but good. He couldn't wait to be finished and on his way home.

As Dario made his way down the floors, working alone a lot of the time cutting and laying plywood over the newly formed holes in the floor he said it felt like he was being watched. He would constantly feel compelled to look around but there was no one there but him. This seemed to happen most times on the 22nd floor near the purple striped stairwell.

One frightening incident happened to me on a beautiful Friday in March. I had been delegated to the elevator job by Lucas. The morning work was going very smoothly. I was looking forward to hanging out with some of the guys at lunch time and talking with Tina from my cell phone. I was walking around the work floor talking briefly with some of the crew and then took the elevator down to bring up five empty wheelbarrows. I would be able to ease into the afternoon after lunch as all the wheelbarrows would be empty. Beautiful I thought. I'll load the elevator, drop them off and take a well deserved break before lunch. After the doors had opened I flipped the switch down, to the service position, to hold the elevator for loading.

I loaded the fifth barrow; 'K boys, lets go it's almost lunch time'. (They were an important part of the team).

I flipped the toggle switch up to the run position. As the doors closed and the elevator started up I looked at the lit up floor numbers above the doors then heard a noise; 'thump'.

One of the wheelbarrows had suddenly fallen forward, the wooden handle pushing the switch down. It was like a dream as I quickly tried to hit the switch back up but it was too late. The elevator had stopped. A feeling of claustrophobia and panic took over as a sudden gush of warm air hit my face. I flipped the switch quickly back and forth, but nothing happened. Me and my orange clad helpers were stuck.

'Oh God, please no' I heard myself whisper as I looked at the vertical line in the centre of the doors. Elevator number two had stopped. This couldn't be happening, what do I do now?

My adrenaline started kicking in like a sudden rush of energy; the fight or flight response. To make matters worse I had about a square foot of space to walk on while the five wheelbarrows were taking up the remaining space. I stared at the numbers on the display panel for what seemed like a long time not knowing what to do next. I was internalizing the worst. What could be the worse scenario? Dying.

I'll never forget thinking that I was going to die but I didn't know why. People got stuck in elevators all the time didn't they? Surely they'll notice I'm in here and rescue me some how right? I'll pry these doors open if I can, I thought.

So I braced my weight into the doors to try to open them. 'Aaarrrggghh.' I was pulling as hard as I could but the doors barely moved. I managed to get them open a couple of inches but that was all.

'What the heck is that,' I thought to myself. I was stunned at what I saw in the small opening in the doors. My heart went faint as I realized my odds were getting worse. In front of me was a concrete wall! That didn't make sense to me at all as my mind scrambled to figure out why I hadn't seen in between two floors while trying to open the doors, like a scene in a movie. I took an inventory as to what tools I had with me to help my situation. On the floor of the elevator there was nothing. Out of all the many tools we had on the site such as crow bars, I had nothing except for five orange wheelbarrows. I forced the doors open a couple more inches and yelled out.

'Help, I'm stuck in the elevator'.

I pressed the alarm button and let it ring on and off for a minute.

'Silvio I'm stuck in the freaking elevator', you out there, hey Silvio'.

I remember hanging my head feeling defeated and thinking panicked thoughts like would my air supply run out or not. It felt like I couldn't breath in there. The air was thick as I tried not to worry and stay calm.

'Silvio, anybody. Can anyone hear me, I'm in the elevator, get me out of here'.

I remember thinking; Oh God, I don't want to die. I'm sorry Lord I shouldn't think this way.

I told myself I was going to be alright but my panic and anxiety grew stronger the longer I was in there.

What time was it and why hadn't anybody heard me?

I did another round of buzzing the alarm. My watch read ten minutes to noon. I started hyper ventilating and used my shirt to help with my breathing. I noticed a bit of water in my bottle and drank the last sip. My face felt warm and got to the point of being uncomfortably hot like it was on fire. I had never been stuck in an elevator until that day. I guess it's something that crosses everyone's mind, but being stuck in one is a surreal intimidating experience. I was finding out what it was like and it wasn't good especially in this creepy building. Finally I heard what sounded like Silvio call my name. Finally some help.

'Hey Silvio I am stuck. Get me out'.

He said something but I couldn't make it out, it was all mumbles.

'Silvio, I can't understand you speak louder'. I could barely hear him.

'What floor are you on?'

'What floor am I on, I don't know there's a block wall in front of me. I can barely hear you'. Just get me the hell out of here. I'm worried I will run out of air.'

'Just take it easy. Do you have the switches in the right position?'

'Yes, just get me out of here.'

Silence again. I couldn't hear anyone or anything, just an oppressive silence.

I switched the air to its low setting. I thought; Is this really how I'm going to die, in this old elevator with five orange wheelbarrows?

When I heard Silvio tell me he was going to have to call for elevator service I knew in my gut I wasn't getting out as soon as I wanted to. After a silent prayer to God I noticed I was slowly calming down. I checked my watch again noticing it was twelve fifteen p.m.

I couldn't believe how this had happened. How could the wheelbarrow just fall on the switch like that, it seemed impossible but I watched it happen.

I could barely hear people talking to me on account of I was stuck in front of that thick concrete wall. I was yelling to be heard, so I tried to relax and turned the air on high and tried to control my breathing.

I started thinking that I shouldn't feel afraid. Thinking of what those poor people went through in that fire was what instantly came to my mind. This was nothing compared to the horror of going through what they did. I'd be okay and hoping that helped me feel calmer and grateful that I was still alive and would probably be rescued. At least I wasn't dangling up on a higher floor. If I fell I'd probably survive.

Apparently most people can survive a five floor fall in an elevator but not much higher and I was stuck between the 2nd and 3rd floors. That fact helped me feel better, more optimistic. Then I thought to look for the escape hatch on the roof of the elevator. The orange barrow would come in handy if I had to crawl out. The thought of being stuck in here for the night made me even sicker with paranoid thoughts. This place was crazy enough during the day; being trapped in here at night would be a nightmare.

'Get those thoughts out of your head' I told myself; 'Don't get yourself going for nothing.'

It's amazing how powerful the spirit of fear can be.

As I sat there I felt powerless. It had been almost an hour being trapped so I decided to climb the wheelbarrow and try to open the small opening in the roof of the six by eight box. It wouldn't open. It was locked on top for safety. How ironic I thought as I realized I would need a crowbar or sledge hammer to open the escape hatch so, so much for that idea. I was trapped. Nothing I could do but accept the reality and wait. I was thinking how oppressed and helpless my spirit felt being confined. My biggest fear was running out of air.

'Exi?' It was Silvio. 'The service man is here, he is going to have to let you out from the top. He can't get the elevator to move. He will have to climb on to the roof and open the escape hatch'.

That didn't sound very safe but I knew I was happy this nightmare was coming to an end. I heard the service man opening the hatch eight feet above me and I said; 'Man am I glad to see you, you're my new best friend'.

'Having fun yet?' He asked.

I was too tense to laugh.

'How do I get out of here?'

'Just take your time when you step out. We'll have to carefully walk over on to the other elevator and climb down into it. There is a ladder inside'.

I climbed out onto the elevator roof and took a quick look around. It was dark and cold. I stepped over onto elevator # 3 and made my way to the opening, climbing down the ladder and out onto the third floor. If the floor was clean I think I would have kissed it. Instead I saw Silvio.

'You are my hero, thanks pal'.

I gave him a grateful hand shake. He chuckled and said;

'Don't thank me thank Cliff, he called the service man'.

Cliff was the manager of the operations of the Parks Sets Motel. I walked over and thanked him.

'How was it in there?'

'Just brutal, I am so glad to be out of there.'

I yelled a 'yee haw' as I made my way down the grey striped stairwell to the main floor and walked down the hallway outside to have a cigarette. The blue sky and sunshine was so good to see. I noticed Roy sitting on some concrete slabs and went over to thank him for his support. He asked me how I got stuck so I told him about the wheelbarrow falling over onto the switch, stopping the elevator.

'Felt like I was done for when I realized I was stuck between the second and third floors right in front of that concrete wall. It felt like I was going to run out of air and my face started burning up too. It was creepy in there'.

As I walked to my truck for a late lunch I decided not to let Tina know about my latest adventure until later.

I drove out for a coffee at Tim Horton's™ then came back and tried to eat some food. As I replayed in my mind my ordeal, I decided I would be taking the stairs for a while and see if the elevator would get stuck. I didn't need to experience that again. I saw Silvio after lunch and I let him know that I wouldn't be working the elevator for the time being, if he could let me work on a floor just to take a break. I joined the crew on the 12th floor.

As the days went on I noticed the middle elevator had not been repaired. They couldn't get it going again for more than a month and when it was operational it was extremely slow in closing and the buzzer would go off until it closed. It didn't open any faster either.

They were old and caked with dust and being over used with all the renovations going on. As I continued researching the motel, I read in one of the articles that on the night of the fire the heat was so intense it had melted one of the three passenger elevators. It said the heat was so hot it stopped the number one elevator and melted the quarter inch thick steel. It stopped on the seventh floor. No wonder that elevator was sealed off from use. I guessed they had probably had issues with that elevator ever since. There must have been massive warp damage to it the night of the fire.

We were all sensing an oppressive heaviness at work. It was as if something negative was all around us; a stuffy feeling; dirty, evil. Silvio told me that the service man couldn't figure out how the elevator could have stopped exactly where it did, in the only section of the creepy climb in the tower that was surrounded by a concrete wall. I had been stuck in front of the second storey of the second floor which is all concrete. The odds of that happening made me feel ill at ease. Silvio made it a rule to carry our cell phones, especially while working the elevators.

I made up my mind to trace my foot steps on the 24th floor and debunk my first video once and for all. I figured if this video of the same area had a white shape in the window then it was always there anyway, probably a fire hose. If the white form was no longer there then this place just might be haunted. There were plenty of bizarre things happening around us for sure.

Dace and I were left to finish the 11th floor so at break time I got more footage of the room on the 24th floor on which I had seen the reflection from the window of something white. I took the stairs, considering only one elevator was working. How would someone get out if there was a next time? A person couldn't be rescued if the elevator doors were shut. With no second elevator to crawl into you would be trapped with no way to get to you for a long while. Marvelous.

After taking another video and reviewing the footage at home, Tina and I both saw what we knew already, and actually it's what we didn't see that astonished us. There was nothing white. Nothing there at all. That innocent day not so long ago, I had video taped a man in a white dinner jacket. Tina was as amazed as I was.

'How could that white thing be a man, Tina? There isn't any one at work walking around in white let alone a dinner jacket'. That must be a ghost!'

Then Tina said; 'you know that a ghost is oftentimes a demon, a fallen angel right Exi?'

'That's a pretty freaky surreal way of thinking', I said, 'but I think you are right. But why me? There's no cause and effect really, why are we the ones after all the years the spirits have been there, why are they bothering us? Something's telling me there are at least two spirits in that tower'.

I would soon find out there were more than two ghosts at the Park Sets Motel. A lot more. Still, I was excited at the reality of working in the haunted tower. I was feeling intimidated too, this was a different type of spiritual battle my co workers and I were experiencing. We would joke about things at work but I think all of us felt on edge working in the tower.

Something that surprised me was showing up for work one day and noticing that one of the floors had been demolished the night before. The cinder blocks all around the floor making up the inner hallways were sledge hammered, left in piles. The ceilings were knocked down and the plaster hammered off of the interior steel meshed walls. Someone had thought of bringing in a night shift to help get caught up on the increasing workload at the motel.

I had heard a worker had seen a ghost and at first I thought they were making fun of it. I asked him what had happened. He was sure that he did see a white figure at around four in the morning of the previous night. He was going down the main floor hallway to the rubble pile for a break when he saw a white shape floating at the bend. Then the shadow moved down to the exit door and vanished into the night air. It would be a real thrill to see stuff like that at night. It gave me a chill just imagining it.

By now I believed there was more to this motel than meets the eye. Dace and I were working on the eleventh floor early on finishing the odds and ends. I was pulling nails out of the ceilings using my two foot step ladder for the needed height. That's when I noticed I was falling backwards onto the concrete floor. I braced my body for the impact and luckily fell on my side. Dace saw this happen and walked over to see if I was alright. We both realized I hadn't lost my balance. We knew deep down that I was pushed. I had to laugh it off it was such a surreal incident.

Matt was one of the workers who thought it was funny to sneak up on us to scare us. While Dace and I were working on a floor I remember he snuck up on me while I was working in front of the three elevators. All of a sudden I noticed something to my left. I froze while staring at this crawling creature with nylon panty hose on his head. I knew it was a human and as it came closer and wailing; 'oooohhh', I realized it was Matt.

'Nice try' I said, as he laughed hysterically. It was pretty funny.

'You're a pretty brave guy making fun of stuff like this, but be careful man you don't want to annoy them if they're here. I'm serious.'

He got a big kick from it all. He asked where Dace was and I crouched with him sneaking around the corner until we saw Dace. I stayed just out of sight so Dace couldn't see me as I watched Matt sneak up right behind him. Dace turned slowly as Matt wailed, crouching like some ghoulish creature. There was no reaction then a brief chuckle from Dace as he realized it was Matt.

'Skipper, you kill me man, hey, hey, hey'.

The prank left me on edge.

'Pay backs are a drag' I said, as Matt wailed then disappeared around the corner and down the grey striped stairwell.

There's no way I was going to tell these guys, not even Silvio about the spirit I saw on video. I'm sure they were already nervous enough. But I needed to share this with someone who might be able to give me some feedback and insight as to what was going on in this motel tower. It was draining at times dealing with the haunting on my own.

I found a paranormal research site from the city area and sent out an email explaining some of the activity at the motel, and asking if anyone would be interested in talking with me to help me rule out the possibility of a haunting, though I knew in my gut, in my spirit by this point that something very odd was happening. We agreed to meet at a coffee shop on a Thursday night of the next week.

I was also forming a habit of collecting keepsakes from the Park Sets Motel. We were allowed to take things home since it was all being thrown out anyway. I thought it would be nostalgic to take home one of the few unscathed telephones I had found that used to hang halfway down the wall beside the toilets in the former motel rooms. I brought one home in a plastic bag. I would never try to use the phone; I just wanted it as a souvenir, a memory of the job site.

I showed Tina the phone and she didn't seem to mind me having it. My intention was to put it in storage, but for the night I left it in the hall closet. That evening I watched the eleven o'clock news and went to bed feeling content.

As I drifted off to sleep I noticed a set of eyes, red eyes, beady eyes staring at me.

'Tina'? I had to check if I was dreaming.

'Huh, what is it Exi?'

'I don't know what's happening but I just saw a pair of red eyes staring at me.'

'Maybe you are just over tired. You've been working pretty hard lately. Maybe have a cup of tea. It might help you to sleep.'

As I tried to forget the image of the red eyes, I was falling asleep again when I saw in my mind, a woman running through a smoke filled hallway frantically brushing away the smoke choking her as she searched her way around. Then I heard an audible voice say;

1} "BRING IT BACK; BRING BACK THE PHONE, NOW!"

'No', I screamed out.

'Exi wake up, you're having a nightmare'.

As I lay there shivering I told her; 'I don't think I was dreaming. I am so creeped out right now'.

I sat up and I told her what had happened, then decided to check our balcony. I checked and came back inside.

'It seems like I was attacked in some bizarre way, Tina. I'm not crazy, you know me. I wasn't having a nightmare either; I was awake. I'm bringing that phone back tomorrow. I don't want to keep the damn thing. Something is pissed off. I was visited by a spirit just now and it was on the balcony, I really think it was I could sense it there, like I do at work'.

After putting the phone on the balcony I asked Tina to pray with me for protection. I tried to sleep again but I couldn't after experiencing that so I got out of bed and made some tea. I was awake a couple of hours thinking back on everything and now the red eyes of insanity coming from the gloomy tower. That poor woman I saw choking in the smoke kept playing over in my mind. It brought tears to my eyes. And now with this spiritual attack I was really going to pay attention to things at work. I was convinced that whatever was there didn't like me, but I had a right to be there too and I decided to fight back however I had to.

At this point I couldn't wait to meet up with the guy from the paranormal site. I was hoping he would be someone who believed what I had to say. Maybe he would know why 'they' were harassing us.

What he suggested I do from now on at work would change how I understood the world around me. It would scare me to my core too. And just how much of a power struggle between good and evil there would be in that creepy place was yet to be played out.

1} masculine-voice

Chapter Three; Are You Talking To Me?

2nd Corinthians 11: 14 -15 *And no marvel; for Satan himself is transformed into an angel of light. Therefore it is no great thing if his ministers also be transformed as the ministers of righteousness....*

After kissing my sleeping wife's cheek, I grabbed my cup of coffee and the bag containing the phone I had brought home. The whole experience I had last night was too bizarre. It left me exhausted and feeling drained. As I drove to the haunted tower I wondered how many other people in the world were dealing with a haunted work site. There must be some for sure. Ever since I saw the video of the white shape on the 24th floor, I felt on edge more times than not. Last night was too much, too weird for my mind to make any sense of it. As I relaxed in my truck parked beside the towering motel I gathered what I needed for the day and grabbed the bag with the cursed phone. I needed to return this bag to the third floor where I had found it under the sink.

The spring sunshine felt soothing as I locked my truck and stared into the healing rays before entering the tower, walking through the back service area like many times before. Somehow the air felt a little thicker today. The concrete giant was always damp and cold with only heat from the wall heaters on the main floor hallway. Even though most of the workers still took the only working elevator, I took the grey striped stairwell to the 3rd floor. I put the phone back where I had found it. I felt relieved.

I eventually made my way up the stairs to the 11th floor where Dace and I had been working finishing odds and ends, while the others were a floor or two below us. I walked around the floor, opening the twelve sliding windows. The fresh air seeped in, replacing some of the stale air trapped in the tower. For different reasons I believed this place was haunted. I was on guard from that day on and I have to admit I was feeling pretty intimidated.

Knowing your enemy in a battle is important but all I had was a blind faith in the strength that God would give me to deal with whatever came my way. I was prepared for almost anything. What other choice did I have? I wasn't going to let some invisible entity control my life. I knew that it wasn't from God.

As the days went on I felt more and more detached from my co workers. I never felt comfortable with any one at work knowing about the apparition I had filmed upstairs. We talked about a lot of different things and for sure we talked about the past fire and the nine people dying and about the unusual things happening to us but I never shared my findings with them.

I didn't want to rock the boat. As time went by we pretty much just accepted that the Park Sets Motel was more than a creepy place to work.

The weather was mild the April night I met Don from the paranormal society. It was a Thursday so I was pretty worn out, not only physically but I was emotionally drained as well. I parked at the coffee shop we had arranged to meet at and felt a sense of relief knowing I would be sharing my haunting with someone outside of my circle. Though the spiritual attack in my apartment not long ago had terrified me, I wasn't going to let some ghost tell me what to do. I also kept collecting odds and ends I was finding in the motel. I just didn't bring them into our home. Looking in the back of my truck I noticed my growing collection was scattered around.

Maybe Don would want to see the souvenirs; maybe he could pick up on any energy that might be coming from the articles. I noticed a vehicle coming in and thought it must be him. As he parked along side me I noticed a woman in the passenger seat and assumed it was his wife.

We bought coffees and went back out to sit in our vehicles.

'So first of all tell me a little bit about yourself'.

'About myself?'

'Yeah have you got a family, married?'

'Uh yeah married but no kids yet my wife's name is Tina. And what's your name?'

'Danielle'.

'Nice to meet you too.'

'Have you ever experienced anything before?, he asked. Don't feel embarrassed'.

'Oh, no I'm not, my wife and I are Christians although we're not fanatical about it'.

'No no I understand, interesting so you're Christians very interesting'.

'Well you gotta be something, I think'.

'For sure that's fine I don't have a problem with that. So what you have seen then you may not think is, well I don't know I'm speculating.'

'Well I'm still kind of putting all the pieces of the puzzle together too and it's very uh, it's very what's the word I'm looking for, subtle?'

'Well Exi, if it's any consolation to you, I've been doing e.v.p. work for quite a number of years'.

I had never heard of that before so asked him; 'And that stands for what again?'

'Electronic voice phenomena. I kind of fancy myself as a kind of out of the box thinking kind of a guy.'

Don said that he had an electronic technical background, that he was an electro mechanical repairman. He went on;

'What I have found from the e. v. p.'s that I've gathered, believe it or not backs up what the bible has to say. It hasn't shaken my faith its re affirmed my faith in Christianity just by listening to these e.v.p.'s.'

'Wait till I tell my wife that, I said. Have you done a lot of that stuff in the area; is there a lot of this stuff around here'?

'Oh yes, I did one recently in Kingston too. That one was interesting. I got some really good stuff there. It was the Hagar house. I've heard that Bounder Castle might be haunted as well. I've done the Merckley house and the Dwight Theatre.'

'That is so neat, I said. Have you heard whether the Kane Mansion is haunted? One of my co workers mentioned that him and his wife have eaten there and weird stuff happens'.

Don said; 'Yes I have heard about it. I tried to find it once to investigate it but couldn't find it'.

Then I asked if he had heard about the Park Sets Motel or of any reports of hauntings and he said I was the first person he had heard from about it. He also said it wasn't unusual to have paranormal activity at a motel or restaurant.

'Did you do your own research about the history of the Motel?' he asked.

'Well I thought the building was interesting when we started renovating it, so I went on line and found out about the fire. I'm working in a different atmosphere than I'm used to. I feel more apprehensive thinking about the activity while I'm at home like I know there's an extra obstacle at work, but at work I am focused and alert and not fearful. Something spiritual is happening but it is confusing'.

I explained about the videos I had taken and the image in the shots. The newspaper articles revealed where in the building the nine people had died. Of the nine deaths, seven had died in the purple striped stairwell, and two died on the 24th floor, coincidently where I had filmed the apparition.

'I took the video and noticed the apparition before I knew about the deaths'.

I told them the white figure looked like a man in a dinner jacket. I explained about the activity I knew of that the different workers at the motel tower had experienced and told them of the attack the night I brought the phone home. He asked if I had returned it.

'I did but I grabbed another one'. That made us all laugh.

'I did. I have a number of things but now I leave them in the truck'.

'What else have you experienced'?

'Well I've noticed a number of times while working, the feeling of someone or something looking or staring at me, so me and some of my co workers feel the need to look around to see if any one is there but we never see anything. That feeling of being watched usually happens near the purple striped stairwell which is also the area where we feel our ears being flicked'.

Don then explained that some studies have shown that electro magnetic energy can give off the feeling that you are being watched. He also said that the research is now being questioned.

'Good to question', I said.

'And don't feel silly', he said. 'I grew up in a haunted house so I know'. Don't be scared to tell me, because I know'.

'No I'm not that's okay', I said. My personal belief is that there is at least one hostile spirit in there'.

'What makes you feel that it is hostile'? He asked.

'I felt like I was pushed off of a ladder one day last week while me and a co worker were working on the eleventh floor. It was kind of a floating feeling. I've been working for many years and never had that happen. When my co worker noticed I had fallen he came over to see that I was alright, and he mentioned he saw me going over and it seemed to him that something had pushed me. That surprised us both.

Then Don said; 'The only evidence that I truly believe is paranormal at this point is electronic voice phenomena. I have over forty tapes at home with examples of e. v. p. on them. Have you noticed any 'place memories' at the tower which would be something like, a maid walking down a hallway or a butler or something like that'?

'Well, I said; that thing that was standing behind me on the 24th floor sure looked like a waiter to me. The room I took the video in isn't a room where someone died in, but I am assuming that spirits have the ability to roam around and two people died on that floor, they have the whole motel to themselves right? I believe there's at least one angel in there watching over me as well or God knows what would have happened. I also got stuck in an elevator one afternoon, for about an hour. Considering one elevator melted on the seventh floor the night of the fire, being stuck was pretty intense. They are pretty old and creaky'.

I went on and explained my experience in the elevator and how I had to get out through the escape hatch.

Don said; 'I was just thinking of a thousand ways to die'.

As we laughed I said; 'Believe me I was thinking that too while I was in there.'

Don explained that it's not unusual for people to experience paranormal activity during a renovation. When things are changing like that it tends to stir up activity.

'That's very interesting, I said. 'One of the guys saw the elevator lights flickering on and off and that was the same day the washroom faucet turned itself on. My co worker Dace is from Jamaica and maybe superstitious and I don't think he would mess around like that to make it up.

Then Don asked; 'So you generally get a creepy feeling in the whole place right?'

Yes, its got that kind of dreary kind of feeling to it like a thick heavy fog. My wife and I both think that someone who died there at one point was maybe spiritually possessed and some demon escaped from the body and its maybe been there ever since. There's no proof to that but anything is possible. It's just something as a believer in Christ I believe is scriptural'.

'You're right it is possible' he said. It's good that you're looking at things and your going; well is that what I really saw? You're looking for a natural reason. Always look for a natural causation first because you never know how stuff can happen you know? It's good to keep a journal and something else too is keep note of the weather because it can have an effect on our moods'.

'Even things like taking pain killers for a bad tooth or something, that can make you hallucinate and you don't even know it'. I suppose it's not possible to do an investigation in there because there are laws right?'

'Yeah I said; the whole hard hat thing, construction site for safety and insurance'.

'You're right, he said, which is a real shame really but you don't want people in there stomping around falling through a hole or something. It would be great to do an investigation though. That's too bad, for sure'.

Then I asked them; 'Do you have any advice for me as far as what I can try to do, because I want to try something?'

'Definitely, he said; for sure keep a journal. The second thing is, is it possible for you, do you have a little tape recorder? It doesn't matter whether it's digital or tape or whatever.'

'Yes, I said, I have a digital one.'

'Well good. Try and find one with an external micro phone. You don't have to spend a lot of money anything will do really. So try to keep the mic as close to your head as possible, maybe in you're shirt pocket then go through your day having normal conversations with people. Believe it or not some people think that it is better to leave the recorder in a corner or something and walk away but it's not.

Carry it with you and review it at night and if you hear anything that sounds different, you'll hear that it sounds different, like a thump, thump, thump. You might hear cynical phrases too things like, after your foreman says; 'Joe, go over there and start busting down that wall', and then you'll hear someone or something say, it'll sound out of place so it'll go; 'yeah man you start busting that wall'. 'It'll be cynical like that'.

Then I asked him; 'Do you think spirits are more active at night?'

'No, that's not really true. We've collected stuff on bright sunny days that would just blow you away. But on a more serious note I know of a woman who died a few months back. They were urban investigating, not ghost hunting. She fell between a roof of two houses and she died. So you've got to be really careful so we don't advocate that type of thing. I mean some people think you're just plain out nuts anyways, a coo coo.'

'I think I understand Don. I would be interested in hooking up again after the job is done if you don't mind probably at the end of May, as I don't see us being finished that quickly.'

'Yeah, sure Exi. So you think you're going to do some evidence gathering'?

'Yeah I'm going to do that with the recorder for sure. That should be quite interesting'.

And he asked; 'Is there a way that we could get a copy of that video tape? Or if it's private could we just get a section, that one section on the 24th floor?'

I was a little weary of letting anyone have copies of anything at this point and I didn't have it with me anyway so I told Don and Danielle I could bring the video the next time we met up.

'We will not post anything without your permission and it sounds to me like, and I don't want to lead you on but seems to me there is a good possibility that there could be things there. It's not unusual to have a haunting in a motel. I'll give you some insight into it to help you collect your e. v. p. data'.

'Okay sounds good', I said. I was looking forward to anything he could tell me.

'Believe it or not, I have found that spirits don't want to be alone. This is what I have learned personally. Think of if you're dead. You're dead; you're hanging out on earth, okay, as a spirit what do you want to do? You want to do the things that we used to do in life, but you can't do them any more. You don't need a ticket to go to the theatre. You don't need to pay for a meal at a restaurant; you know you don't have to eat.'

As Don chuckled about these scenarios, I listened with great intent;

'See, you took something out of that motel and it's possible something didn't like that so it harassed you about it.'

'Oh yes I believe it was something like that. Here I'll show you some of the stuff I've got here. Here's a phone. Do you get a feel for stuff when you touch them or handle them?'

'I used to be much better at psychometry than I am now; that's what it's called', he said.

As I handed him a phone from one of the former rooms at the motel, I said; 'Here you go. Now it's still got the old dust on it and everything so don't lick your fingers.'

After a few seconds Don said; 'This phone used to ring and was in room 759.'

As we had another laugh we noticed it was a pretty old phone maybe from the seventies.

'I was thinking, after all the smoke damage from the tragic fire a lot of things in the rooms had probably been cleaned up instead of replaced because when we're gutting the rooms I notice all the black soot in different areas on the concrete. The tower is being converted into a rental residence building, so I don't want the spirits bothering those new people.'

Then he said; 'What I get from this phone is all these wild looking carpets with flowers and squares on them. A lot of that old looking stuff.'

'You are right. Your right on wow, pretty good', I said.

Apparently he also got a few impressions of some families from the phone he was holding. I showed him some more of the artifacts I had collected.

'Here's an ashtray, I've only seen one of these.'

'I would hang on to this stuff if I were you', he said.

'Oh I'm going to try to yeah. I've found a few cardboard coasters too real nice looking. I hope to find at least six of them to have a set'.

Don read an old price list for rooms I had handed him; "Wow in 1982 a single room was two hundred eighty five dollars. Yeah that was a five star motel for sure'.

I showed him a key I had found.

'Careful with this one', he said; I think ghosts charge a lot of money for the mini bar eh'? We laughed.

It was a relief sharing my findings and learning so much from their experiences as paranormal investigators. He added;

'What I have found about hotels and restaurants is that I think spirits like to hang out. It doesn't surprise me that you would see things like that and if you did some investigation you would probably find some pretty good evidence there. It would be a really good place to look. I'm not going to guarantee you'll get something; I think you'll be very interested with what you might get with the recordings'.

'Yes, I'm going to try every day if I can,' I said.

'Yeah, he said; when you review it just see if something sounds out of place or responds to questions and you know no one else is in the room'.

'Right on, I said; so I can even talk as if someone is there and see what happens right? I think I'm going to have some fun.'

Then Don told me another of his experiences; 'We're on this road in middle northern Ontario, and I have to say that's another misconception that a place has to look spooky to have activity. So we were on the side of the road doing some e. v. p. recordings, my wife and I are driving and asking questions with a mic at the window and two more on the dash of the car. So my wife says; 'do you like the cold? And I ask her; 'isn't that a silly thing to ask a ghost?' And she goes; 'no', and then says; 'do you feel the cold'? Then all of a sudden you here a voice say clearly;

1} "NA".

'So you had to listen to it later because you didn't hear it at the time?' I asked.

'Right, we couldn't hear it. So you may not hear anything at the time of the recording, you'll hear it later.'

Danielle said; 'The thing is they do respond to you. We've had answers to questions. And conversations; they venture into our conversations. Basically they want to hold a conversation but you'll only get one word, two words or three words at the most'.

'Alright thanks, I said. I've noticed my video doesn't pick up audio very well'.

'We've never picked up an e.v.p. on a video camera, Danielle said. The only thing I have found that gives me physical evidence of the paranormal is an e.v.p.

'I didn't notice the white figure in my video until much later' I said.

'You may not have seen it, Don said. 'My wife and I five years ago recorded our first e.v.p session. We were in a cemetery being respectful, looking at the grave stone markers and I was about ten feet away from her and she snapped a picture and when she did she noticed someone standing in front of her. She looked at me and asked if I had stepped in front of her and I told her that I hadn't. She swore it must have been me and I told her again that it wasn't me. Then all of a sudden after that you hear a very, very clear voice say';

2} "IT WAS US".

'It gives me shivers every time we talk about it', she said.

'That spurred us to keep going and that was five years ago, but that was our first e. v. p. recording we ever got.'

'That is really neat; I can't wait to get started. I guess we should all get going I know my wife will be waiting to hear about our meeting. I will ask my wife to come with me next time. That would be good'.

'Sure, Don said; we would love to review anything you might catch.'

'Awesome, thank you, I said as I started my truck; 'it was great meeting you both and thanks so much for sharing all of that with me. The advice is really appreciated. I can't wait to get started. Take care and watch out for them ghosts, this was really cool'.

'Well at least you know you can talk to someone without being made fun of about it'.

'That's a real blessing Don, for sure. Its been a pleasure; I'll be in touch, thanks again.'

Wow that was great I thought as I tuned in some music on my fm radio. I checked my phone and text Tina that I was on my way. I definitely thought through all the advice Don and Danielle had shared with me especially the possibility of catching voices on my recorder. I would alternate between shooting some videos and using the digital recorder at work. I wondered if Wal-Mart™ carried any recorders so I stopped in and found one for around sixty dollars. That should do the trick I told myself as I arrived home and made the elevator ride to the 7th floor.

Tina was asleep. It was eleven p.m. and she usually packed it in early on work nights, ten o'clock or so. I opened the fridge for something to eat. Cereal it is. I was too tired to heat anything up. As I looked around the half packed apartment I thought of the work still left to do. Tina and I were also moving up a floor in our building to a bigger unit with two bedrooms.

Being married to my best friend is something I didn't think was possible not too long ago. But neither was working in a haunted motel. I thought of an old saying I had heard years ago; 'life is what happens to you when you're busy making plans'. Seems to be.

Tomorrow was Friday and like most nights I was dead tired from my work week and staying out later than I thought to meet Don and Danielle, but it was all worth it. I felt excited to start recording. I hadn't heard of e. v. p.'s until tonight.

Tomorrow I would start a new dimension of what seemed like insanity.

That night I prayed for protection and guidance and reminded myself to put batteries in the digital recorder before I left in the morning.

Trust in God's protection, I told myself. Don't depend on your own understanding with this mystery. Seek His will and He will direct your path. It was comforting to know as I fell asleep that God would get me through this, as He has many times in my life.

Little did I know how much different this direction would turn out to be, so much different than anything I could have imagined. But my faith in God's power to conquer evil, and the authority I believed I had through Him to battle the spirit world, would eventually prove true its weight in gold as I encountered and confronted all the noisy spirits from the Park Sets Motel.

1} masculine-voice 2} masculine-voice

Chapter Four; This Could Be War

James 4: 7 **Submit yourselves therefore to God. Resist the devil, and he will flee from you.**

The next day at work was like any other at the motel tower. I was a little nervous about being there now, knowing that it was entirely probable that the motel had spirit entities as tenants and I got the impression that whatever was there wasn't friendly. During my morning break, I videoed more footage on the 10th and 11th floors. It was a dull damp April morning and it rained all day.

I walked my way up the grey striped stairwell and got out on the 10th floor hallway and started the video. As I walked I zoomed the video in on a pile of cinder block rubble, which had recently been part of the hallway, now destroyed.

I narrated; 'This is all the rubble we have to take down, all this stuff here', moving the camera slowly and deliberately, the footage capturing some final memories of what was once part of a beautiful room. As I made my way along the debris filled hall I was careful to watch my step…

1} "DON'T WORK"…

I video taped the ruins walking to my right, filming each room with only the wire framing of the inner room walls left standing along with electrical wires hanging from everywhere. Some of the mini tiled bathtub walls were intact along with the bathtubs and toilets. The tile floors in each bathroom were left for last being jack hammered off later.

'We have to tear all the metal down all the rubble has to be taken down.'

I kept walking using the narrow pathway in the hall making my way around until I passed the grey striped stairwell then around yet another corner to the front elevators. I turned around and went back, up the grey striped stairwell and continued video taping on the 11th floor;

'And this is what it looks like when it's finished'.

Most of the rooms were now wide open with all the interior walls demolished, allowing all the outside light to brighten up the entire floor, also most of the debris had been collected sitting at the elevator doors as if waiting for someone to wheel it down for disposal.

Dace and I were on this eleventh floor finishing the odds and ends and my not so fond memory of being pushed off of the little two foot ladder was still fresh in my mind.

I made my way into room 1148 just missing stepping on a claw hammer, one of many tools lying around. I made my way over to the windows and continued filming now the outside cloudy view of the damp drizzly day…

2} "GET OUT LEAVE"…

'There's downtown', I said as I scanned the view. I turned around and went to some pipes in the room. 'And here are the pipes that I scratched my arm on.' I turned off the camera and went down to my truck for a sandwich and some water and ate it as I walked up the stairs to the 11th floor. Dace and I continued working on the floor that morning.

During lunch time Silvio noticed all of us standing at the side hallway door talking and finishing our lunch break when he mentioned that there was an important meeting first thing in the morning. Lucas wanted to talk to all of us. As we made our way to the 11th floor we commented our opinions as to what Lucas' talk would be about.

'I hope they will not be laying us off or anything silly like that' I said, as we stepped out onto the 11th floor corridor.

'No I doubt that, Dario said. We're all good workers and if anything we need more workers. There's just too much left to do. Even Silvio told Lucas we needed more people.'

'Yeah bumba clad, they better not lay us off yet, they should be paying us danger pay for having to work in this creepy evil place,' Dace added.

We all had an uneasy laugh at that comment and joked about Silvio telling us about getting his ears flicked on a regular basis while he did his final rounds in the corridors each day. It was the kind of humor that made me think that we had better be careful in dealing with whatever was spooking everyone out.

'It's pretty creepy in here especially when I was working on the 22nd floor by myself. It really felt like someone was watching me up there', Dario said as he laughed.

I guess he was hoping Dace and I wouldn't think he was crazy. Dace and I just looked at each other and then back at Dario. I told him how I was pushed off of my ladder and that Dace had seen it happen, in a fluidic way like there had been something else there with us. Dario laughed nervously, surprised by my story and seemed relieved that it wasn't just his imagination.

I said; 'Hey, I believe you my friend. If you need any help you just come running to get us and we'll all beat the hell out of those ghosts once and for all because there is power in numbers you know what I mean? Anyway how dare they flick our foreman's ear like that! No worries you guys; the Lord is near and He will make us strong and guard us from the evil that's lurking.'

'Amen brother Exi, amen,' Dace said, chuckling as he walked away.

Dario chuckled too as he walked to take the stairs down to the 10th floor mumbling something about how weird this building was turning out to be. I yelled out a 'praise God, thank you Jesus,' as we shook off the uneasy feelings the best we could. Ghosts fear hearing the name Jesus. It makes them tremble. I figured that some of my co workers thought I was a bit weird anyways, but than again, who isn't? I didn't worry too much about that. I was grateful for His protection, and that Silvio had let the others know about the fire and that we all knew a little about the motel's history.

I'm not a religious fanatic but I was using the authority I had in Jesus' name to keep any evil as far away from me as possible. What did I have to lose? I was better safe than sorry. Whatever was here was evil, I could sense it and it wasn't from God as much as I knew for the simple reasons that there wasn't a feeling of peace or understanding and confusion doesn't come from God. I was on edge, ready for anything, staying alert to my surroundings.

I spent most of my afternoon filling barrows with broken cinder blocks and dust then brought them down to be emptied. It gave me the chance to take another video of the 2nd floor which was staying in tact. It was a beautiful looking floor and I sometimes thought of how I would have enjoyed to have been able to stay at the motel and have memories of even one night at this five star rated dwelling. I put the number three elevator on service and walked the expensive looking hallways, admiring the beauty of the Park Sets Motel.

I zoomed the camera in on the two silver plated wall plaques that gave directions to the various rooms and restaurants that sat further in. 'This is the 2nd floor of this magnificent old motel', I said. It was the 2nd video I had taken of this floor and they were in stark contrast to all the others which were pretty beaten down. I took the quick video and then noticed it was quitting time.

The next day I walked up the grey striped stairwell to the 3rd floor lunch room.

The gang was all there; Lucas the boss' son, Silvio our foreman, Dario, Dace, Roy, Rudy, Matt, Papa and me.

Lucas started. 'I guess some of you know why I called this meeting. For those who don't, the main reasons are for safety and if any of you have any safety concerns they should be addressed here today so if anything needs to be done, my father and I can take care of it. Another reason for this meeting, and I am not singling any one out but guys we have to pick up the pace. We're supposed to be out of here for the end of the month. This job was supposed to be finished by then but it looks like that won't happen.'

'Some of you have missed days and not called in and just showed up the next day. Can't do that guys it really messes things up for us so please just call. Even if you have to miss some days, Silvio and I don't mind, just let one of us know. Also we finally got the second elevator going so our trapped barrows are on the fourth floor just waiting to be filled.'

'Way to go Exi', Rudy chirped in. No actually, thanks. It was nice that they were missing for a while. We didn't have to fill em or empty em'.

Everyone laughed. We often ribbed each other, even Lucas which was cool considering how serious things would be at times.

'Even though you're the one who got them stuck in there in the first place, Exi I want you to keep working the elevators when we need containers. I know we are also short of hammers too. Is there anything else you guys need?'

'Yeah man, Roy said; 'we could use more ear plugs and dust masks and I don't like falling behind out there with the Bobcat™. Sometimes I run out of diesel and have to wait forever for it and that messes up my day. Don't make me work up there; I like it outside in the fresh air. I drive the Bobcat™ that's my baby out there that's my job, not in here.'

'You're not afraid of any ghosts are you'? Lucas asked.

'Heck no, I know how to handle ghosts man I stay away from them. I don't provoke them I leave them alone and they better not harass me either that's all I know.'

As we all laughed again, Lucas asked if there was anything else anyone wanted to say.

'Yeah, I said; just wondering if you could get a few more shovels as the Skipper seems to be breaking them all.'

'You just mind you're P's and Q's trouble maker', Matt said as he laughed.

As Silvio cackled his famous laugh we slowly strolled down the hallways and went our separate directions laughing and telling more jokes.

I ventured up the grey striped stairwell alone. All of us liked working solo and the place was big enough for us to do our own thing and maybe the ghosts liked it when we were by ourselves so they could watch us better. I did the usual when I reached my floor. I put all my personal stuff like my keys and phone, granola bars and bottled water some place safe and clean then wiped out my full faced dust mask before putting it on, then put on my safety glasses and gloves; either cotton or leather depending on what work I was doing.

I also ran the elevators often enough to be able to shoot videos. I just made sure no one else was around. It was oppressive being in the elevator by myself considering I had been stuck in the center one, so I tried to take number three elevator as often as I could.

I videoed everything I could including the smoke damage caused by the fire and all the different aspects of the designs in the different rooms; the different stages of the project on the floors and stairwells curious if I would catch pictures and voices of the supernatural.

I recorded the 10th floor again in the afternoon amidst the faint banging and clanging on one of the higher floors…

3} "I'M CRASHED OUT"…

Then I took some footage of the purple striped stairwell between the 15th and 16th floors knowing that one of the men in the fire had died there. All nine had died from smoke inhalation, or carbon monoxide poisoning.

I filmed one of the fire hydrant hose cases near one of the stairwells to see if the wrapped up hose resembled a white suit. It didn't. I videoed elevator #3, showing all the different floor numbers and the laminated brown wood grain design popular in the seventies. I filmed burnt pieces of insulation from the fire, and bits of burnt out cinder block that survived the fire.

At one point that afternoon, I put the elevator on service on the sixth floor and filmed through the opening all around it, filming the shaft areas of the elevators…

4} "LET'S THINK ABOUT IT, WOOMP WOOMP"

As I entered the tower after my 2nd break I filmed the back service area on the main floor near where Silvio let us in in the mornings, and where we left for home. It looked pretty beat up with the painted concrete walls and the ceiling paint peeling away. A long black pipe hung horizontally wrapped in a white insulated sleeve.

I moved my camera around filming the various contents; an old large portable fan, three skids of expensive looking marble tiles and there was also an old hotdog cart on wheels, white and beat up. It reminded me of one of those old style baby carriages from the fifties, the ones with the huge wheels. There was an old mini aluminum fridge standing by itself. I moved over to the service elevator area. The one that had melted that fateful night years ago was cordoned off with the red safety danger tape, with a red spray painted piece of plywood that read: 'Danger. Do Not Remove'.

I moved on to film the dark brown double fire doors that separated the rooms from the back hallways, then I walked to my left down the curved fire exit hallway with red arrowed fire exit signs painted on the walls. This was how most of the people had escaped from the fire that night so long ago. The grey striped stairwell was just back the other way. The grey stairwell exited in this hallway, while the purple stairwell exited to outside to the service bay driveway.

The seven people who tried to escape down the purple stairwell were met by impassable smoke and collapsed in the stairwell and died.

I headed back past the brown fire door to the curve of the hall that jutted right and then left. Right took you fifty feet or so past the grey striped stairwell fire door, then into the main area in front of the elevators where three steps down to the left took you to the entrance of the indoor pool door. Beside it was 'kids play' area room for all the supervised children's programs. To my left the hallway continued into the basements main floor about one hundred feet long, then curved to the right leading to the men's change room on the right. Going straight would lead to a curved hall again going left, but I never ventured down it. It was pretty dark down there so I didn't.

There was no rest for the wicked and I wondered if the camera was catching more ghosts or recording any voices. I had to somehow devise a way for the i.c. recorder to stay safe and clean. I'll figure that out I told myself as I left in my truck to battle the afternoon rush hour.

I resolved that I could keep the i. c. recorder in my pant pocket or shirt pocket with duct tape. I remembered what Don had said about keeping the recorder close to my head. To see how spirits would react I duct taped a cross 8" by 4" in size on the back of a work T- shirt. I showed it to Tina and she said it looked great;

'At least the ghosts won't sneak up on you with that cross staring at them. That should keep them in line.' She could be right. She usually was.

The next day at work started out like most others with Silvio cracking his jokes and his whip. Matt missed work once again. Dario was his usual happy self. Dace was sarcastic and funny as always. I was reserved about it all. We all made each other laugh.

As we changed on the third floor I donned my crossed T- shirt and showed the guys. Most of them laughed, especially Silvio. Maybe they thought I was over doing it or something but we got a good laugh out of it just the same. I felt better knowing my 'back was covered' symbolically at the very least. The duct tape stayed on for a few days and then I'd peel it off, wash the shirts and put more duct tape on again.

At morning break I grabbed the video camera and took some time during the day to shoot more videos. I took elevator #3 to the seventh floor and started filming. The floor was still intact for the most part with only the wallpaper and some of the porcelain and mirrors in the bathrooms removed. The double width square mirror on the wall facing the elevators was majestic; it was nine feet high and eight feet long. I walked left and focused on the first room. There was a silver plated plaque that once adorned the hallway wall, now lying on top of some rubble in the hall just inside the room. A black painted arrow pointed left to rooms 751-756. I kept walking left while getting a good look into each room as I went along.

I went into a few of the bathrooms and took some footage of the phones hanging knee high beside the toilet with some of the elaborate marble and mirrors still in their place. Later in the morning I took a video of the boiler room in the back of the tower on the main floor. Supposedly the deadly fire was unknowingly started by a lit cigarette butt being sucked inside of a small vacuum cleaner and then stored in a closet somewhere near the boiler room. The room had massive multi colored pipes everywhere. A cluttered design like an abstract picture.

After lunch I decided to video starting in the former men's change room. It smelled extremely pungent and moldy in there just like an unused shower change room would smell. It hadn't been used in years and surrounded by the massive slabs of concrete it was like being inside a musty pit in the ground.

In front of me was an old chair. My video scaled the flaking paint on the ceiling scanning to the right, to the wall of a shower stall and a sitting area with an ashtray mounted on the wall directly beside me...

5} "DON'T PUSH ME"...

I turned the camera left, reading the sign on the door; 'Men's Change Room #12'.

6} "TRY THIS ONE" ...

7} "LET'S BE FRIENDS" ...

The basement was like a maze. Pipes ran all the way through this part of the motel lining up along the ceilings zig zagging their way along with the halls to who knows where down there. I walked towards the bend and turned left to record another long hallway. These back hallways were bigger than the floors above them and also formed a parallelogram. Really neat I thought. I enjoyed exploring this huge creepy building.

This place was literally falling apart without any help from us humans. I walked into the men's change room again and scanned the room then turned around walking the short hall and turning right to film from the entrance to the indoor pool. Then I turned to film from the entrance to Le Place discotheque and bar, one of the first discotheques in Canada. It was dark and dingy but with enough light to zoom the camera left and get pictures of what used to be the dance floor and further back up a few stairs was the platform for D.J.'s and live acts. The Rolling Stones had played here once, a stop on their way to becoming famous.

This place was quite popular in its day. Now it looked very shabby. The chairs and tables were stacked and rolled against the walls. The square black tables looked expensive and heavy. I stopped filming and made my way up to my work floor.

A while back I had read an article from the internet about a man who had survived the night of the fire. He alleged he was guided by a man in a suit on the fifth floor to escape the heavy smoke, down to safety via the passable grey striped stairwell. The article stated no one could figure out where that man disappeared to that night or who he was. Some people figured maybe he was really an angel. Maybe that's the spirit I filmed on the 24th floor. Maybe I would film him here today.

As the elevator opened I put it on service and started filming the fourth floor. The floor was still mostly intact. The large double mirror in front of the passenger elevators was still there as well as the plaster room walls and hallway cinder block walls. The wallpaper was stripped off and all the carpets had been thrown out. I made my way left and filmed the hallways, then the grey exit stairs and the pitch black room where the two back service elevators are then took footage of the purple exit stairs before coming full circle to the mirror again.

8} "WHAT THE F*#K?"

Then I took the number three elevator up to the fifth floor for more recordings.

I zoomed out and saw 545- 550 painted in black on an orange wall to the right of the big mirror. Going right took you to those numbered rooms. I took video of the foyer area near the passenger elevators, turning slowly while recording to take it all in…

9} "WHAT'S UP FOOL"…

I finished recording and took the grey striped stairwell up to meet Dace and finished work for the day.

The next day at work Matt and I walked through the back and took the elevator to the third floor along with an old man. He was small and thin and didn't speak much English, just a few words. We nodded to him as we got off the elevator and went to the change room for the regular morning laughs.

'Who's the old man?' I asked Matt as we put our work boots on.

'I haven't the foggiest idea but he looks just like the little dude on the Lord of the Rings, Sméagol is the characters name so that should be his nick name. Have you seen the movie, do you know who I mean?'

I almost choked on my coffee as I laughed.

'Yeah Skipper, that's too funny brother, I said; I'm just going to call him chooch. I'm not trying to be disrespectful but he looks like a chooch to me'.

'Chooch, too funny Exi,' he said as we laughed while walking to the elevators.

'Sméagol' was inside number two elevator and said, 'you go up'? We said yes as I pressed the 9th floor button. That's where Matt, Papa and Dario were working. We got off on the ninth floor and I walked to the stairs to the left, to the grey striped stairwell and climbed to the tenth floor where I met up with Dace. The floor was almost finished so we were pretty content today, not feeling so rushed with the handful of extra workers helping to try to get the renovation back on track. Dace and I were efficient workers so we knew we were doing our share.

Break time brought another opportunity to video tape. With more workers at the motel I left my voice recorder in the truck and focused on video taping instead. It has audio too so I hoped it would pick up some voices. I took elevator number three to the 24th floor. When I knew no one was around I started the camera. I wanted to take some shots of room 2468 where one of the victims had died in their room. I started in room 2469 in front of the elevators, and then scanned right filming the double length window view with the winding stairs to the 23rd floor then turned left and walked the hall and entered room 2468. I felt apprehensive but filmed the room for a few seconds then took the elevator back to the 10th floor.

At lunch time I decided to get a longer video of the 25th floor, or private floor suite 500. They must have had some pretty wild and expensive parties on these upper floors. The view was spectacular up there. The floor had six balconies about forty feet long. This floor is twenty feet high and had spacious offices and the private balconies. I noticed that two sets of stairs went higher than this floor so I started my climb. I was in the grey striped stairwell and took my time, going slowly watching not to trip in the dimly lit landings. Since the 25th floor is a double high floor like the 2nd it has a '26th' floor with various mechanical rooms, generators and exhaust fans, utility rooms and various exits to the roof.

I reached the 26th floor doorway and walked through the short hallway out onto the 26th floor.

10} "GET OUT"…

'Oh this is wild', I said. A door was on my left some sort of mechanical room.

I filmed it then turned around and kept walking ahead noticing the windows along the outer shell of the exterior walls. Each wall had ten windows, about two by five feet in diameter imbedded in each of the six walls forming the perimeter. They helped give it the tower look I thought, like a medieval castle. I turned right into the first room. It was high, maybe twelve feet, rectangular in shape and there was black soot everywhere, dark as night. The big metal vent in the upper corner wall was allowing daylight in from the roof otherwise the room was pitch black and dark. I continued walking going right until I came to the purple striped stairwell. I climbed the stairs up into the pitch darkness just noticing a splinter of day light coming in from what seemed like a roof access door. I turned around into total blackness then down the stairs and took a right into another small rectangular room with pipes hanging and a chute door for whatever. It was creepy black in the chute. As I turned right I went through to another smaller room with a door leading to part of the roof. I tried the steel door but it was locked.

As I walked back to get to the elevators I noticed soot splatters on the inner block walls.

During my afternoon break I ventured back upstairs to the 25th floor. I wanted video of the back elevators that I had forgotten to film earlier. When I was back on the 10th floor, Silvio approached me and told me the old guy was Hectors brother and starting tomorrow he would run the center elevator, while Matt and I would alternate using the other one in an effort to get more done.

'They are going to send some of you downtown to help rip out some carpets for a few days; I think probably Dace and Dario, and maybe you too. I will let you know tomorrow.'

'Okay bud, I said; 'I hope it's not me. I would rather stay here.'

'You want to stay here with the ghosts?' he asked.

'Sure man I don't mind, if they bother me I will come and get you. I will scream for help but you have to come to help me okay?'

Silvio laughed; 'Yeah sure man, you are crazy man you had better leave them alone or they will flick your ears.'

'No worries buddy, we will use our martial arts me and you just like in a movie.'

'Ha ha, he said; okay man no problem but do me a favor and make sure the windows are closed around quarter to four okay?'

'Any thing for you my friend. I think you are the real boss here or you should be, you're a good man Silvio.'

'Okay Exi whatever you say see you tomorrow.'

It would be nice to get out of this motel for awhile, but I would rather stay here instead of break up my routine. I took some debris down to the first floor in the elevator and Rudy took the wheelbarrows out for me.

I noticed Dace standing there.

'So what are you up to tonight? Are you going to watch the hockey game, the Montreal Canadiens™ are going to win the game I feel good about it.'

'No man, I have to go drywall tonight, need the money know what I mean I need to see more green bro.'

'Hey I hear you brother my money isn't tight but it ain't right either I need to win the lottery. See you tomorrow bro don't work too hard buddy.'

'Alright big chief see you later.'

Big chief. That was a funny thing to say.

The next morning I was determined that I would use my audio recorder more often.

When I arrived at work I secured my recorder with duct tape to the inside of my pant side pocket. When I was ready all I had to do was press record. This would be interesting, an adrenaline rush. I walked past Roy as we said good morning and made my way to in front of the elevators. I was ten minutes early so I sat on the company water cooler by the elevators, relaxing and drinking my coffee until Silvio would show up.

I figured since it was so quiet it would be as good a time to start recording as ever so I pressed record and let it run. As I sat and relaxed I looked around into the kids play room with all the motel furniture from the rooms stuffed inside it, and some kids activity posters still hanging on the walls and ceiling.

11} "HORK PLEASE."

"HUMPH, HUMPH, HUMPH, HUMPH, HUMPH."...

"OKAY".

It felt good just to sit, relax and reflect on my life and on working at the motel. Eventually I heard footsteps coming toward me, someone's hammer clanging against metal coming from the back hallway.

'Good morning buddy', I said. It was Dace.

'Yo buddy, heh, heh, heh.'

'I shot the sheriff but I did not shoot the deputy', I said, to get him laughing.

'Yeah hey, hey Rastafarian, I shot dee sheriff, but I did not kill thee deputy, hoo, hoo, hoo'.

We got into the elevator and Dace said;

'Yo dog, we shall work until twelve o'clock today on the dot.'

'I know bud that idea was beautiful', I said.

'I don't want bumba clod people spoiling our day dog'.

'Yeah man I hear you.'

I laughed as we got off on the third floor. He was venting for us being reprimanded the other day for taking different lunch breaks. Dace was funny even while complaining.

'Yo Silvio, what's happening', Dace said as we walked over to him.

'Morning boss' I said.

'I'm not the boss', Silvio said chuckling.

'Well maybe you should be. Where do you want me this morning number nine, number eight, number seven?'

'You finished number nine?'.

12} "I'M NOT DONE YET"

'Pretty close', I said.

'You go to number nine Exi and I will send another guy.'

'Okay buddy'.

I walked to the elevator and noticed a new shovel with a large plastic scoop light weight but heavy duty. 'Hey Paco is it okay if I use this'?

'Yeah', he said.

Silvio overheard us talking and came over to tell us it was the last dropped ceiling but the sixth floor had bulkheads all around the hallway. He asked Dace to start cleaning up the eighth floor.

Three of us got in the #2 elevator. I pressed the button eight then nine and we took the elevator up.

'Up and down, up and down,' Dace said; just stick to one floor and just kill one floor'.

'I agree brother,' I said. The elevator went to nine first.

'Wow that's weird, I said; it's not supposed to do that'.

Papa got out and the doors closed beeping as they did. It went down to eight. We waited for the doors to open.

'What the hell' Dace said. He pushed the button a few times; 'Yeah it's stuck'.

"Not again,' I whispered.

The memory of last month's horror of being stuck in this box for an hour by myself came rushing back. At least I wasn't alone. All of a sudden the doors opened. 'Oh thank Goodness, that freaked me right out' I said.

We got out on the eighth floor.

'Now I have to go up by myself.'

'Be careful man', Dace said with a high nervous chuckle.

I almost went back up by myself to appear brave about it but quickly changed my mind.

'Forget that man I'm not going in there alone'.

He started laughing; 'You don't mess with the ghosts, eh? Ha, ha, ha, hoo hooo'!

He had a good laugh. I took the stairs to the ninth floor.

I made my way to one of the window ledges in a room to place my belongings out of the way of the work.

There was plaster everywhere covering the ninth floor hallways about six inches thick. I grabbed a shovel and a wheelbarrow and made my way over to near the elevator foyer and started shoveling the heavy plaster.

I heard the elevator bell cling and Chooch came out and watched me work for awhile asking me questions and making comments. For the most part, I couldn't understand what he was saying so I just nodded yes or no. He looked around a while then walked around the hallway circling his way back to the elevators.

13} "DON'T GO FOR ONE DAY"…

14} "WHO'S THAT THERE?"…

I was extremely tired that morning not really looking forward to clearing the floor. It was a disaster but I dug in realizing it had to be done.

I heard Paco working on the other side of the floor continuing from where he had left off yesterday. Then I noticed Rudy near the elevator;

'Hey Rudy are you going down for a shovel?'

'Yeah I'm going to take the wheelbarrows down you want one?'

'Yeah that big plastic one please, thanks buddy.'

He took the elevator down. It was noisy for awhile with three of us hammering. Then it stopped. It was quiet and peaceful as I waited for Rudy to return.

15} "A HUMAN"…

'I'll shovel the big stuff into wheelbarrows for you k?' I asked Rudy as he handed me the shovel.

'Alright', he said.

The morning dragged on like I thought it would. Papa was busy dismantling interior walls in a room while Paco was taking down wire mesh on the hallway ceiling after hammering the plaster off and I was going around putting different piles of the debris into containers and barrows. We were almost finished the floor by four o'clock.

The following week at the motel I was left to finish the ninth floor alone. While Matt was helping Silvio on one of the upper floors the other guys were on the eighth and seventh floors and Rudy and Roy were working downstairs and outside.

The past weekend I had been reading through some of the newspaper articles I had printed from the internet about the fire and decided to get some video footage of the purple striped stairwell, hoping more spirits would be photographed.

I took my digital camera up with me on the Thursday of that week, and at break time started filming the stairs from the 22nd floor down. I went up using the number three elevator and filmed the rooms as I walked to my right. As I got back around to the elevator I flicked the service switch off and made my way to the purple striped stairwell door. I opened the door and started my way down.

I breathed heavy through my mask as I descended the stairwell a little uncomfortable realizing seven people had died in it. As I got to the fourth then the third floors I shut off the camera and took the elevator back up to the ninth floor.

I met up with Dace later on at the elevators to go downstairs.

'It's almost over eh?'

He just stood there like a zombie looking half asleep. I felt bad for him. He had worked last night and was dog tired.

'Yeah' he said.

'Later bud' I said.

'How you doing there?' a voice from behind us said.

'Hey there Dario'.

'I'm gonna pour these barrows out, he said; I know it's taking awhile'.

'You're a good man Dario', I said, as we chuckled. I knew the haunting was keeping him on edge.

We all went to the seventh floor after lunch. We all did our own thing. I was prying the wooden slats of wood off with a flat scraper that the carpets used to be tacked to.

16} "WHO PUSHED THE CHIEF?"...

One thing I did a lot of in that motel was walk.

17} "STOP"

18} "WHOA"

I could hear the other workers doing some type of work. It sounded like an orchestra some times. Sometimes it seemed to blend in sequence. I banged on some duct work…

19} "THAT'S COOL"…

'This is hard work' I said to Papa.

He chuckled and said, 'I am just pacing myself'.

'I'm sweating Papa what's up with that'?

20} "IT'S NOT SWEAT."

I needed a break so I knelt and rested.

21} "WHO'S ASKING YOU?"……………..

22} "PUT THAT BACK HERE"……………...

23} "HAVE MERCY"…

I saw Dario and asked him; 'I guess the old guy is gone home?'

'Yeah Matt is running the elevator. He's probably having a smoke outside or something'.

'Gotcha it's all good bro.'

We took the elevator down for our lunch. It was soothing to eat my wife's wonderful cooking and relax and enjoy the sunny day for a while before going back up into the tower.

The afternoon went well and we ended up getting a lot done.

'Hey Dario is that your tool belt'? I asked him.

'Yeah yeah, I got a new one', he said.

'I wouldn't leave that here overnight, I said; in case some ghost picks it up and puts a curse on it or something.'

'Yeah hee, hee, yeah right, he said; what about the stuff you take out of the scrap piles Exi, you just never know'!

It was fun to joke around but maybe there was some truth in what we were talking about.

24} "NO PROBLEM"…

He told me a story about a couple of paintings he used to own and sometimes when he came home they seemed to be moved out of level. There could be a logical explanation but you never know I guess.

'That elevator melted on this floor, like thirty one years ago.' I said.

'Wow, he said; 'I wonder why they don't have service to it right now, because it died'?

'I think its probably been warped ever since, something goofy like that', I replied.

'Yeah when those bigger flames are going that melts everything', he said.

We gathered up the tools and waited by the elevators. It became a ritual that the person in the elevators at quitting time would stop on the floors and pick everyone up. The doors opened up.

'Ready guys? Silvio said; let's go home.'

Matt was inside working the buttons. Dario asked him where he was going.

'I gotta check for the other homies man.' He said.

'The mother hen syndrome', I said.

Dario and I started laughing. The doors opened on a higher floor for the other guys in our crew.

'Yo', Matt yelled out. The doors closed again.

'Do me a favor Matt, Dario said; stop on the fourth floor I have to get something.'

'What did you forget now? ' he asked.

'Some grappa Exi brought me'.

'Grappa! You're not going to drink it tonight get it tomorrow'.

I had brought Silvio and Dario some home made grappa that Tina's father had made. He is Italian and has enjoyed it with his coffee for years. At 68% proof it was potent. Matt was always in a hurry to get out of the motel at quitting time.

'No, no, no, because it might disappear, I'm bringing it home 'Dario said; I 'am' going to drink it tonight.'

'Yeah yeah we'll see, hurry up.' Matt said sarcastically as the elevator doors opened to the fourth floor.

'I can drink you're grappa don't worry about it', Silvio said.

'No that's okay', Dario said; just give me a minute to look for it.'

As Dario looked for the glass flask I had given him earlier, Silvio told me;

'I am going to do something to the grappa and I am going to give you some'.

'I guess it is too strong right?, I said; 'I don't know anything about that stuff how to make it or whatever' ….

'Hey, hey, hey', Silvio laughed.

'My father in law soaks green grapes and cherries in his grappa too, those I like', I said.

'Dario? Silvio called for him; you can take the stairs down its only one floor'.

We descended to the third floor and wheel barrowed our tools to their room.

As Dario entered the room I took the opportunity to tell Silvio about the 'dream' I had experienced on the night I had taken the telephone home.

'It really freaked me out. I slept like a baby the next night. Whatever was attached to the phone somehow seemed to attack me. Just take it home with you and put it in a closet in your house and see if anything weird happens to you okay? I am just curious.'

'Is that true'? Silvio asked Dario.

'Yeah that's what he told me. Take it home and see what happens.'

'Wow, Silvio said; a couple of weeks ago I thought of something, like if anything happens to me I'm going to light nine candles, because nine people died. The next night I had a dream that things are happening at work. The next day I checked at work and things were happening exactly like in my dream; the guys working and this and that. The next night I burned eighteen candles not nine, now I am okay.'

'So now you are fine', I asked him.

'Yes, now I am okay'.

'Oh good, I said; so take the phone home and see.'

We all laughed.

'Any of you guys want to try it, its right under the sink'.

'Not me'. Dario said.

'It's true, Silvio said; if I need protection, I light nine candles and put them in the window.'

'Very interesting, I said; see you tomorrow boss'.

'I am not the boss', he chuckled.

'Well you should be,' I said back.

I left as they were talking and headed home for the night. The atmosphere at work was positive some days. It was easy looking forward to coming to work with how smooth things seemed to go at times. I planned to get more video the next day, and this weekend I would be able to download all of the footage I had been taking over the last couple of weeks. I hoped I had gotten more spirits on film. I alternated using the video camera or used the audio recorder for possible terrestrial voices, or e.v.p.'s.

The next day I started filming at lunch time, filming the outside back of the tower from my vehicle and then went upstairs to film the 24th floor again. It seemed to be one of the floors that were most active for paranormal activity. As mentioned earlier, at least two people had died on the floor from the past fire and maybe some suicides over the years had happened on this floor as well as on others. The outside base of the motel tower's perimeter is lined with field stone mostly light browns and grays with a few black and white ones here and there, the wall wrapping itself halfway around the tower to the back entrance ways and lining the second floor hallway. I zoomed the camera close and scaled the side of the tower the video peering into all the windows of its bulging twenty six floors of concrete and glass rooms, slowly becoming a shell of its former self, inside at least.

It was a beautiful sunny spring day as I went in and once again filmed the 24th floor, walking to my right through the curving hallway.

25} "OH GOOD IT'S THE VIRGIN PLAYING"…

I concentrated on being close to the windows in the room I had filmed of the white shadow the month before, to maybe capture another image.

Before leaving for the day I filmed the outside of the tower from the side parking area then walked around to the second floor hallway with the long row of windows facing the rubble pile we were making, where the large outdoor pool used to be. I started filming at the service driveway and walked to my right along the wall leading to the side entrance.

I filmed the second floor where the ballroom is as I walked past the old dusty Bobcat™ parked beside the wall and scanned across the rubble pile to the other side of the motel, its wall of windows leading to what used to be the tower's smaller sibling.

I scanned to my left and filmed the long windows that formed the first and second floor hallways.

26} "CHECK IT ALL OUT"...

I shut the camera off and walked to my truck and drove home in the bright sunshine looking forward to relaxing with Tina, another work week finished. After dinner we downloaded the videos we had shot from many weeks of family get togethers, a few weddings, our old and new apartments and a lot of videos from the motel.

I went through the work videos on Saturday night and I was amazed to see that I had captured more images from my video of the 24th floor in the same room as the white shadow, except this time the images were just heads floating about four feet off of the floor staring back at me.

One face looks just like batman's black caped face with the two pointed ears sticking up except this mask was white with two beety black eyes looking back at me. The other figured face seems to be the same face but it moves to look around so the facial features change. It was the creepiest movie sequence I filmed so far. As Tina and I reviewed the video over and over, we both knew that I had better be careful working in this tower. I remembered thinking that it was a unique way to make a living. I never thought in my wildest dreams that I would ever be exposed to something this bizarre. It was so surreal it felt like I was in a movie and everyone was just acting, the ghosts in particular. I was confident in my faith in God's power, and not my own. I could sense that I needed protection to be safe from any evil lurking in the tower. I believed these beings, whatever they were, were mostly evil because they had demonstrated they wanted to scare us. Something sent from God does not try to scare people. I kept on guard at work; it was a most unusual feeling like having invisible enemies. It was a threatening environment.

That Sunday night as I painted some baseboards with semi gloss enamel, I got the idea that I would paint a cross on the back of my work T- shirts instead of the duct tape. I used a one inch foam paint brush and painted a white cross about eight inches long and four inches across. I let them dry. They looked great, they really did. The semi gloss paint was permanent too so it wouldn't wash off. That should surprise any spirits wanting to do me harm as I believe the cross is one of the most intimidating symbols to evil spirits. It should help keep them away. At a safer distance at least.

I still felt intimidated but I decided I had no choice. I wanted to keep this job so I had to deal with these spirits and if I saw one or heard one speak, oh well. I would just have to deal with it the best I could. I had the will to act. What to do when the time came would hopefully come to me.

I had to go back up to the 24th floor. There was a fair amount of activity up there and I wanted more video evidence. I felt in control and tried to plan ahead. I was also able to take some time to review some of the audio recordings that had captured some whispers and many voices.

It numbed me when I thought about it all especially when I was at home. For whatever reason I felt more intimidated and anxious at home than I did at work. As soon as I would arrive at work most of the fear I felt dissipated.

I was gathering all of this proof of the haunting at the once beautiful motel, now being stripped of its inner glory. The ghosts at this grand motel were stirred up and I'm sure they knew that I knew about them. It would be more than an interesting experience in the coming months. It would also be a dangerous one working around all the filth in the musty old tower.

1} masculine-voice 2} masculine-voices 3} masculine-voice 4} masculine-voices 5} masculine-voice 6} masculine-voice 7} masculine-whisper 8} masculine-voice 9} masculine-voice 10} masculine-whisper 11} masculine-voices 12} masculine-voice 13} masculine-voice 14} masculine-voice 15} masculine-voice 16} masculine-voice 17} masculine-voice 18} masculine-voice 19} masculine-voice 20} masculine-whisper 21} masculine-voice 22} masculine-voice 23} masculine-whisper 24} masculine-voice 25} masculine-voice 26} masculine-voice

Photo of spirits on the seventh floor. Three apparitions are standing near the darker doorway.

↑ ↑

One of the floating heads I filmed. Looks a bit like Jason from the Friday the 13$^{th™}$ movies, or even Batman™ wearing a white mask. Also a bald head above the white area.

Chapter Five; I Will Survive

Psalm 34: 7 *The angel of the Lord encampeth round about them that fear him, and delivereth them.*

As my co workers and I carried on with the ritual of knocking down a floor at a time, the pace quickened somewhat with everyone doing their part in getting caught up so the company could meet whatever their obligations were in completing the project.

Nobody bullied anyone around. Nobody that is except some of the ghosts that were hanging all around us. They were here there was no doubt about that. I can't think back to one person on that job site who didn't believe the place was haunted. We were all experiencing the activity. Whether anyone else was gathering proof of it like I was I didn't know.

In my spare time I started forming the habit of going over any audio recordings I had saved. I would have to go over hours and hours of recordings and write down on which numbered recording and where on each counter a whisper or voice was heard.

Something I was grateful for was with all the video and audio I had managed to record, I had only heard one audible voice with my own ears and that alone scared me. I never did notice any of the numerous photos of entities the digital video camera had caught until I reviewed them at home. I doubt I could have handled working in there for very long if the ghosts would have appeared to me or spoken at a level that I would have heard them.

From what I've learned about hauntings it is common to capture images of spirit beings in pictures only after taking them. This is called 'spirit photography'.

The theory of the phenomena of e.v.p.'s is that voices and whispers are caught on a higher frequency so a person generally doesn't hear the voice at the time of whatever it is that's trying to communicate. They were all new experiences for me and I was totally fascinated that I was experiencing the haunting upfront, personally and literally. Some of the activity going on around me was literally 'in my face' just as Don had mentioned.

That week most of us were on the sixth floor and now that we were all pretty familiar with the tower and what needed to be done the work day usually went pretty smooth. Usually.

One day I was shoveling up the larger debris of the smashed up cinder blocks.

'Hey Exi', I heard a voice say; 'see that sweater? 'It was hanging over here, Dario said. 'When you walked away I figured nobody was there. Out of the corner of my eye I could see it.'

I said; 'I think you've had too much caffeine brother.'

'Yeah, he chuckled, yeah maybe but you know out of the corner of your eye, your peripheral vision when you think you see something?'

'Oh yeah I know what you mean', I said. And I certainly did know what he meant.

Everyone seemed to be in a good mood with the sun shining and being grateful for a feeling of solidarity. I was also grateful that I wasn't always working alone.

'One more round to go', I said to Dario.

'We've almost got it knocked off now', he said

'What's up boys?' we heard someone say. It was Lucas. 'Did you miss me'?

He walked around in a good mood stopping to talk to some of the guys. Dace saw Matt and me in the hallway and came over and said;

'He's crying like a baby cause it's taking too long.'

1} ... "POOR BABY"...

'Show us the money bra', he said as we all cracked up.

2} "IT'S A JOB DON'T WORRY"...

The rest of the afternoon went well, I remember it was one of the few days that didn't feel as oppressive as most. Dace and I met up at the elevators and took a quick break.

'Another day almost over dog another day completed, done', he said.

'Rain shines on the just and the unjust, the sun shines on everyone', I said.

'That is beautiful, beautiful', he said, as we chuckled.

Dace also wore a cross, on a chain around his neck.

'What do you think of this cross I painted on the back of my shirt; check it out man near the bottom it looks like an image of that shroud of Jesus they discovered years ago'.

He looked at it and chuckled.

'Bumba clad, you kill me Exi'.

Dace and I seemed to have the most fun mocking the haunting. I was glad he was working here at the motel. We seemed to know when to take each other seriously and when not to.

'Another day in paradise brother Exi, Exi, paradise.'

'Could be a lot worse', I said.

'Oh I know', he said. 'You've got that cross on you're back so you're alright,' he said as he started to laugh.

'They don't like that eh, they stay away'.

'Yeah I know, yeah bro', he said, showing me his cross. We sure knew how to get each other going. It helped to take the edge off of the creepy feelings that were often felt around us. We knew they were here.

Matt, Dace, Dario and I were loading the wheelbarrows and wheeling them to the elevator doors so that Sméagol the older man could take them down to Roy. I was told that 'Sméagol's' real name was Bablo and he was the boss's brother, but we called him Chooch or Sméagol because those two nick names stuck with us. We were getting ahead of him bringing empty barrows back up and sometimes waited awhile for him to return.

Bablo came back up with a couple of barrows and slid them part way across the floor knocking down a push broom along the way.

3} "PICK IT UP!"…….

"NO"…………..

"HOW"…….

"I DON'T KNOW" …………… "ACHOO"…

As Lucas walked past me I said; 'Have no fear the ghost busters are here okay?, me and Dario'. 'We have Bill Murray on speed dial'.

He smirked a laugh and took the elevator downstairs.

I filled up some empty barrows then decided I would start asking the spirits some questions so I went up to the next floor to get away from the noise and the rap music playing. I took the stairs to the landing, pressed record on the machine and said;

'This is hard work heh?' …... 'What do you think?'…… 'Why are you guys here anyway?'

I grabbed a shovel leaning against a wall and filled more barrows with debris.

4} "NOT BAD THIS KIDS CLEAN".

'I'm breaking my back bro', I heard Dace say.

'You are strong like a bull, I replied.

'We're here to make money bro', he replied; 'you know what I mean'?

He hadn't noticed me recording the air in the tower.

That week at work I took videos of the 24th floor again at the windows where I had filmed a reflection of the floating heads looking back at me from behind where I was standing, across from the purple striped stairwell.

I took the stairs down to the main floor and drove to get coffee for my morning break. I listened to News Radio in my truck during break then walked to the side entrance and made my way to the elevators. I pressed the button and got into elevator number three. I got out on the third floor and made my way to our lunch room where some of the crew was talking.

Dario and I talked about one of the extra workers who had been working at night who claimed to have seen a white shadow in the main hallway. We wondered whether he was making it up. Neither of us was sure but I was leaning more toward believing him. If it was true, I thought of how creepy it would be to see a ghost at two o'clock in the morning in the still of the night in the musty old motel. I had asked Lucas earlier in the week if he would be willing to allow a couple that I knew to come in and investigate the motel for any paranormal activity. He told me he would think it over but he never did get back to me about it. I asked if I could work some nights instead of days but the work at night was stopped because some residents in the area were complaining about the noise and the dust.

We all got up and walked to the elevators. Sméagol took us up to the floors.

I stepped out and went to the coolest part of my work floor, one of the rooms near the back elevators and took my keys, cell phone and water from my pockets and placed them on one of the window ledges. In the background I could hear Dace coming up the stairs.

'It does all good owe, ooh, ooh'.

I replied with; 'Owe, ooh, ooh, ooh'.

He walked over and said; 'How are you Exi?'

'I'm good bud how are you?'

'I like that grappa, he said. I took some from Silvio and tried it the other night, strong stuff man'.

'Corona is all I drink', he said. 'It's expensive though a two four is near forty five dollars, bumba clad'.

'Yeah but it's worth it. I'd rather drink quality beer if I'm going to drink. Some of the cheaper beers taste pretty nasty. I don't like a lot of them.'

'I hear ya bro', he said as he turned and walked to the room he had been working in.

5} "YOU STOP HIM"………. "MAYBE I DID" …

As I cleaned up some broken glass I could hear Rudy laughing with Dace in the background. As I shoveled I separated any metal from the piles of crushed cinder blocks then filled the wheelbarrows. I saw Dario coming around a corner wheeling a barrow to the elevator so I took my mask off to take a break from the dust and I continued one of our on going conversations.

'It doesn't scare me but its new phenomenon for me you know?'

'Well, I haven't said anything to anyone but when I was standing over there it's like this ear, I literally felt something touch it a couple of times'.

I could see by his face and by the tone of his voice that he wasn't kidding around. He just confirmed to me again that the spirits were moving all around the tower.

'You probably did feel that then', I said. 'I don't know about you but I noticed this place has like a gloomy bogged down kind of a feeling to it. I've heard that's a sign of a possible haunting as well.'

'Yeah I do know what you mean', he said.

'Hey Dario, if you want to you and I can uh, go up to the top floor and do a form of cleansing on this place'.

'No, no I keep away from that', he said.

'I really don't want to do it by myself.'

'Yeah, he said. I just don't want to. I don't want to bring it home with me you know. It's just my own conscience you know what I mean? It's just not something I want to do'.

'No, no my friend that's cool', I said.

As he walked away I felt a kind of regret that I had brought it up. I didn't think it would upset him but maybe it had somehow. As I continued shoveling he walked back and we both made sure we were okay about our last conversation. He was okay with it which was a good thing. After all, we had to work with each other and wanted to get along. He explained that something like that would just be too intimidating.

'That's alright' I said, and I totally understood. It wasn't something that I was familiar with either, doing an 'exorcism' on a haunted motel. It wasn't something I was planning on doing that's for sure. It was more of a spontaneous thought, something to bring up to talk about.

'I don't want to rock the boat. We don't have all the answers and it's a crazy world you know', he said.

'I agree. I guess I don't want the new residents moving in here to be haunted either though'.

'Yeah maybe you're right', he chuckled.

'A form of exorcism could drive them out of here. There would probably be a big difference in here afterwards'.

'Oh yeah I believe it, sometimes you never know right?'

'It's just like a battle, I said. Sometimes it's good to know what your enemy is up to'.

We were both on the eighth floor while some of the others were on the seventh.

We were being split up more and more as time went on so we could finish off each floor sooner. I was still hoping that I would be sent to a floor by myself so I could take more videos to just set the recorders down and let them run.

I noticed Dace was back on the eighth floor and Silvio was talking with him along with Bablo.

'Inside, the guy is trying to fix the elevator the middle elevator number two. And he says we cannot put it on service so for now no garbage. The thing you guys need to do is find something to do. There is a lot to do up here so you guys just find something to do while we're waiting that's not too difficult right?'

'There is no more rubble'? Matt walked up to me and asked.

'No not right now I guess. The service guy is here trying to fix the middle elevator it's not working at all now'.

'Now there's just this one', Matt said.

'I know. It's pretty weird the way I got stuck in there that's all I have to say about it all.

Then Dario said; 'You know what I heard; when you're not looking for it, when you have no idea you're more inclined to have an encounter than if you're sort of seeking, say if you're walking around knowing, you might not'.

'You may be right that makes some sense', I said.

'I'm interested, he said; 'but it is weird this floor has given me some sort of weird aura…

'You hear that? Even though it's just the wind it's weird'.

'I hear you bud. You's are messing with Dario and me now', I yelled out.

He laughed and added; 'not me man!'

As we continued working I commented that someone had told me that when there are renovations going on in a restaurant or motel or where ever, some spirits can get stirred up somehow.

'Yeah that's what I've heard too', Dario said.

About an hour later Silvio told us that the elevators were back in service.

'Back to the grind, back to shoveling thanks a lot Silverado'.

Silverado was his new nickname. Dace had come up with that one.

I finished scraping and noticed Bablo had brought up more barrows.

I saw Dario and said; 'This place reminds me of a Stephen King movie or something.'

'I agree', he said as he laughed.

The next day as lunch ended, I shut my truck off and walked over to the side entrance. Roy was there finishing his break, enjoying the suns rays.

I walked down the hall toward the elevator. Lucas was there waiting for it to arrive.

'What the heck is wrong with these elevators? Could be a ghost, some paranormal activity going on in here'.

'Why?, I asked; have you seen or heard anything goofy'?

'No, he whispered. Now the elevator on the other hand it'll stop on a floor, open and shut then go again, open up and, there's nobody there'.

'It usually stops on the second floor for me, I said. I think the place is haunted'.

'I wouldn't doubt it. I think everybody feels it'.

It took a few minutes for the elevator to arrive. The center one opened and Sméagol pushed some empty barrows out then the three of us rode to the third floor as Sméagol and Lucas talked about the progress of the job.

I made my way up to the fifth floor and noticed Dace was wiping his mask.

'Hasta la vista baby, he said; a la vista baby'.

'I'll be back', I said trying out my Arnold Schwarzenegger imitation. At break time we made our way down and rested in the nice weather to enjoy the fresh air.

As break ended, Dario walked over to me and said;

'The ghost wants to talk to you'.

'Yeah that's okay bring it on, I'm ready'.

He was being sarcastic and I was half serious.

'Ghosts don't scare me too much', I said. If he only knew.

We all walked to the elevators and got in making our way back up into the tower. As we got out on the floor I said;

'We should have at least two weeks left in here I would think.'

Dario said; 'I was talking to Silvio the other day and he said they might be adding more work in here'.

'Oh, that would be fine with me Dario. The longer I can be here the better, just keep working and make some more money'.

Just then Silvio surprised us; 'Hey I caught you guys', he said, then laughed. 'Thank you for the grappa', he said to me.

'You are welcome my friend. Just make sure it is good beer you bring me, okay'? 'Dario found his little bottle it's not broken or anything'.

'And no you can't have it', Dario said to him as he chuckled.

Silvio walked away and the rest of us tackled the debris on the floor. I was working in a room just to the left of the elevator corridor and as I faced the hallway and worked on snipping some metal from an interior wall, I noticed a black shadow walk by. It startled me because Dace and Dario were working on the other side of the tower. I left the shovel and walked around to where Dace was.

'It feels like jackson is here today', I said.

'Jackson, who is jackson?' he asked.

'The ghost'.

'I don't know I don't feel he is here, maybe he is sleeping', he said sarcastically.

I didn't tell him about the shadow.

I took a few full barrows down to Rudy and brought a few empty ones back up with me to the fourth floor. Then I brought two more full ones down again, the elevator stopping first on the second floor again as it did on a regular basis. It was truly creepy when that happened. I did that for a while, bringing full barrows down then bringing them back up empty. Lucas was talking with Rudy by the elevator as I entered the foyer.

'I keep telling everybody who is using their head phones to make it so they can hear me other wise if something happens, you know what I mean? You can't hear anything else going on around you'.

He saw me and said; 'I was downstairs talking to Rudy about this and had to tell him to put the stereo volume down so you can hear me'.

'Holy cow Exi; what the heck was that?'

I chuckled at his question and asked him what was what; 'You mean the air from the window'?

'No, no, no, no,' he said.

'A shadow or something?' I asked him.

Lucas was staring out with a weird look on his face.

'What happened man?' I asked again. A couple of the guys laughed waiting for Lucas to talk.

'Did you see a ghost?' Roy asked him.

'No… No, no, no, no. I swear to God I saw a shadow in front of me coming from behind me from a glare on the light'.

'I thought I saw something too just for a split second,' I said, pointing to where I was working earlier. Then Roy, Lucas and I entered the elevator.

'Yo, what the heck', Lucas said.

'I actually saw one like that too, up here on Friday,' I added.

The elevator went down …

6} "HA, HA, HA, HA" …

6} "THAT LUCAS IS STRANGE" …

'That breeze was just weird, (yeah weird eh?, Roy said) and then I seen that. It was like a shadow' …

6} "HA, HA, HA, HA, HA" …

'That's why I was looking behind me then I saw this thing on the wall and I know my shadow is right there and it's something else. I mean what the hell'.

'The ghost on the fifth floor, you've heard of that one right?' I said.

'Oh f*#k off man', Lucas said. He was truly freaked out.

'Ha ha, ha, ha, ha', Roy laughed; 'I'll tell you, this guy is crazy bro', he said motioning my way and as they strolled down the hallway toward the exit talking, I heard Lucas let out a big sigh of relief.

I left a full wheelbarrow of debris I had brought down in the hallway and then went back up in the elevator.

7} "HOW DO YOU KNOW"?

"IT'S ON THE CLOTH AGAIN"

"IT'S NOT TIME TO GIVE IN"…

As the doors closed I thought of everything that had just happened. I knew it. This was just more confirmation. I had seen a shadow earlier.

Lucas' experience had confirmed again for me that no matter how surreal things seemed to be getting, this sad motel had ghosts as tenants. It was too much of a coincidence that Lucas and I had both seen shadows.

I believe all of us were being scared and intimidated in different ways, each of us coping with the haunting and the attacks in one form or another from the entities that called the tower their home. What ever just happened to Lucas was a warning sign to me that the spirits were trying to scare us and maybe they wanted everyone to know it. Maybe now that they were exposed they had nothing to lose by trying to communicate with us. Maybe they wanted to and it was all just part of a game to them, that's what I thought, that to them it was all a funny game.

I decided to start making it a habit to try and talk out loud and to ask questions, to make comments and to see what responses I could possibly record. I felt uncomfortable but did it anyway.

I pressed the button for the fourth floor. I tried to think of what to say. When the doors opened I stepped out and said; 'jackson, what do you want. Were you sleeping or what?'…

Dario was coming around the corner.

'I think jackson just woke up'.

'Jackson', he said in a puzzled voice.

'I think he was sleeping, that's what I named the ghost'.

'Oh okay I see', he said laughing.

I dropped off the barrows and took two full ones down.

'Take it easy jackson. Have a blessed day', I said as the doors to elevator number three closed…

8} "WE LIVE IN HELL"…

As I was leaving the full barrows on the main floor I noticed a figure behind me and to the side. It was Rudy checking his cell phone text messages.

'It kind of scared me seeing you there'.

He laughed without looking up.

'I think I drank too much coffee today', I said.

He chuckled again as I loaded the elevator with more barrows…

9} "LOOK AT THAT……GO BACK".

When I reached the fourth floor I took a walk around looking for full barrows to take down. The floor was about half finished with broken cinder blocks still lining the hall half way around the floor. As I placed a wheelbarrow in the elevator I sang with music I was listening to on my I pod.

As I stepped out onto the main floor, Lucas was telling Rudy about his ghostly encounter. Then Rudy told him a story.

'Yo a few weeks ago I was washing up in the washroom and noticed this light in the hall there was out. I came out a minute later and it was on. I swear to God the light is back on. And I'm here right and nobody passed me the whole time I'm there. No one passed me. I'm like screw this place bro, I'm going outside to wash up now'.

'Hee, heh, he, he, he, he', Lucas laughed, as he got in the elevator with me going up to the fourth floor.

'Maybe that breeze you felt was from the elevator,' I said.

'Yeah, he said; that was from the elevator but that shadow was weird.'

'Oh it was the shadow thing', I said.

'Yeah man. It freaked me right out, it was something behind me.'

'Well, maybe it got in here with us it was tired of taking the stairs.'

'It's following you because it can't touch you', he said.

'Yeah, I said; 'he saw my cross and flipped out and he ran away, that's what happens right?'

There was silence until he gave me a confused expression, which made me laugh more.

'Oh who knows', I said. 'Wearing the cross can't hurt, know what I mean'?

We laughed as he made his way around to talk with the other guys. I kept busy separating some debris and filling a barrow with some broken blocks then got in the elevator again…

10} "EXCUSE ME"…

As the doors closed I said; 'It's warm in here. You freaked out my boss jackson'!

I wheeled a barrow into the main hall and then walked through the back hallway to outside. I lit a cigarette.

Finishing my smoke, I walked back to the elevators.

11} "HOW'S THE BOSS?"…

I loaded up the empty containers and made my way back up. Everyone was quieter than usual today maybe lost in our own little world each of us sensing things just didn't seem normal in this old motel. I tried to think positive but I also kept my guard up. It felt thick in there. It almost always did actually just in varying degrees. I headed back down and dropped off more debris.

12} "DIE FROM IT"….

I filled the elevator with more empty barrows and pushed the button.

The doors opened and I slid the barrows out onto the floor and noticed more full ones.

Dario was on a roll, working like crazy today. He wheeled a full one over.

'Hey buddy there you go', he said.

'You guys are speeding up eh. Come on slow down' I said jokingly. The elevator descended.

Rudy was at the entrance area to the elevators as the doors opened.

'Smells nasty in here', I said to him as he kept texting one of his girls, 'Like moldy or something', I said, as he looked up.

'Probably from the water', he said, pointing to the indoor pool down some stairs to our right; 'all the dampness'.

'My eyes are burning. Maybe the ghoulies are taking a swim,' I said as we laughed.

I loaded up the elevator and headed up for what seemed like the thousandth time. I brought the guys the empty barrows.

Dace looked like a navy seal marine or ninja with his respirator mask on his face and his small shovel and dark clothing. As I walked around I saw Dario using the power grinder on one of the wire meshed walls still hanging in one of the rooms. I started shoveling listening to the music playing on a radio in the distance …

13} "WHO'S WORKIN HERE?"…

After an hour or so I worked the elevator again with my recorder still going and dropped off two more barrows downstairs. When the doors opened Lucas made some weird sound from around the corner that he thought was funny, that he thought would scare me.

'Yeah nice try.'

'Who, who, who', he laughed as we got in the elevator. 'Everybody man don't want to be attacked'.

'What's the score boss'? I asked him. He had something in his hand

'These are big cherries I found outside. The ghost comes around the corner, like a cherry bomb tap! I whack em'.

'It's good that you like having fun at work', I said; 'some bosses are just too serious. But you didn't really see a shadow up there did you. You're just pulling our leg right?'

'No I'm serious I did', he said.

'Come on man. Get a grip will you' I said as I laughed.

As we got out Lucas said; 'I just wish it wasn't me that's all'.

'Yeah I bet', I said. 'Actually I'm kind of envious. I wish it would have been me…On second thought actually no maybe not I take that back, ha ha ha'.

As Lucas walked away I had a gut feeling that he had seen the shadow. He was kind of playing it down with humor but there was nothing wrong with that. Using humor to relieve reality was good especially in this oppressive place.

As I took the elevator down I said;

'Beat but not defeated'.

And I did feel beat up working in this place over the months. This place was trying to wear me down. As I made my way back up, the elevator stopped then opened and Lucas got in. We rode in silence to the third floor.

14} "I DIED"…

Then I went up to the fourth by myself and made sure the windows were closed. I drove home stuck in the afternoon traffic.

The next day at work wasn't any easier than the last. Today would be one I wouldn't easily forget either, and I have the scar to remind me of it like another souvenir to add to my collection of artifacts I had rescued from the Park Sets Motel.

The day started out as usual walking into the tower with its heavy thick aired feeling and the stale, musty smells that permeated the walkways and floors. The sixth floor was where I was working, along with Papa and Rudy. They were working their way down the floors hammering off the glued on tile floors in the bathrooms in the now demolished rooms. All the heavy cinder blocks had been removed and about all that was left were those tiles, the toilets, some smaller pieces of metal wire walls still attached to each other and most of the pipes going vertically from the top floors to the bottom, and horizontally connecting in the rooms.

Silvio sent me to the sixth floor to collect any bulk debris still there and put it in piles or barrows to be brought down. As I got myself organized I took the grey striped stairwell up to the sixth floor.

As I walked to a window ledge on the shadier side of the floor I thought of how tough this work really was and how well all of us were holding up. We were a tough bunch of workers. I thought of Dace working some nights hanging heavy sheets of drywall then working here during the day. He put them up by himself to boot. Silvio worked pretty hard too. He was a smart man and treated us with respect. He wasn't a bully either and he tried to make us laugh with his sorry jokes throughout the day.

All of us worked hard; even the Skipper picked up his pace. And despite the fact we were in a haunting it seemed that we all still had our sense of humor too.

I developed a habit of opening most of the windows first thing when I reached my work floor to help let some of the musty smells out of the tower and let some fresher air in. It was getting hotter outside as the days of summer crept in and inside the tower the humidity was high and the lack of a breeze on most days made it feel like a sauna.

I finished opening the windows then stood by one of them sipping the last of my coffee, gazing out at the serene view below. It looked so grand, so peaceful and relaxed out there. I was on the inside looking out. I was tired and sore but got myself motivated and started working.

Grabbing the pair of snips I had brought up I used them to cut away at the small sections of wire still attached to sections of the floor. I spent the morning cutting and making small piles of folded up wire mesh. I shoveled the different materials into piles and generally worked at a slower pace giving my body, mind and spirit a bit of a rest. You can only push a machine so far before it breaks. I wore ear plugs to help drown out the jack hammering noise on the floor. After lunch I noticed Matt on the sixth floor cutting the remainder of the wire so I decided to go around to the rooms and gather the ceramic toilets into wheelbarrows and bring them down and outside to the large garbage bins.

There were usually twelve rooms so twelve toilets with some still intact and some cracked and broken in pieces. I wheeled a barrow from the elevator corridor and walked around the hallway to the farthest two rooms. I grabbed the ones still intact and hoisted them up one at a time into a wheelbarrow. They were heavy filled with dust so I was just able to get them to clear the side of the barrow as I lifted them in.

I put two toilets in each wheelbarrow and that way I could bring four downstairs at once and it would only take three trips.

After two trips down I started loading the last of the ceramic pieces of the broken toilets and shoveling the rest. I noticed one last toilet. It was still intact but the bottom of the base was partly broken off. I leaned down and tried to secure it. I stood up to try for a better grip. I noticed Rudy was standing close by picking up debris. I thought of asking for his help as this one was a little heavier from more debris stuck in the bowl.

But I didn't ask for help. I figured I didn't want to bother him as he was busy and I had picked up all the rest of them alone. Forget that I thought, I'll do it no problem.

I put my leather gloves back on and grabbed the bottom of the base with my left hand and wrapped the bowl part way around and against my right arm.

I lifted from my legs the safe way and stood up.

Then the toilet shifted down to my left wrist. I felt a quick slicing motion across the inside of my wrist. I quickly dropped the toilet and instinctively grabbed my left wrist with my right hand. My work gloves were still on.

Rudy saw me standing there holding my arm and he heard the toilet drop and asked me if I was alright.

'Not really. I think I sliced my wrist open. Can you go and try to find Silvio for me Rudy I would appreciate it.'

'Sure Exi. Hold on I'll go look for him'

I stood in the room, just standing there feeling the stinging pain and watching drops of blood slowly drip on to the floor.

Oh God no, this can't have just happened. It was too surreal. I started feeling weak in the knees and thought of if I was going to die. I knew I could only loose so much blood before passing out. My thoughts started scattering as I slowly panicked with anxiety. I had to get out of here and try to get some help, fast.

I looked down on my glove and squeezed it tighter hoping to stop as much blood from leaving my body as possible. I looked around but didn't see anyone.

I thought; Is this really how I'm going to die, here, like this? My thoughts and perceptions were dull as I walked towards the elevators and noticed Matt sweeping up some debris.

Am I going to be stuck in this dark hole with these demons? The thought of it depressed me and scared me at the same time. I felt weak and nauseous.

I walked towards Matt for help. He saw me approaching holding my arm. Since we were accustomed to pulling pranks on each other, when I told him I had sliced my wrist and if he knew where Silvio might be he didn't believe me.

'Really man' I said, as I decided to lift my right hand and see.

The glove on my left wrist was saturated with blood. As Matt looked at my glove the expression on his face changed from a smile to shock. He just looked at me staring with a blank expression.

'Where the heck is everybody'? ….'Forget this', I said as I pressed the elevator button, then walked to the grey striped stairwell, wobbling as I made my way to each floor looking for someone to help me.

On the fourth floor I found Dario sweeping and told him what had happened and asked if he knew where a first aid kit was.

'There's one on the third floor' he said. 'Come on I'll go with you'.

'Thanks. I'm feeling pretty weak. I might have sliced a major artery'.

As we got to the supply room Dario looked around but couldn't find the kit.

'I know I saw it here the other day', he said, rummaging around.

'Have you looked at it yet?'

'Not really, I've just been compressing it to try to clot it'.

'You should look at it. You'll probably need stitches at least'

'I can't believe there's no kit here', I said.

Little did I know that Rudy had found Silvio and he had taken the kit up to the sixth floor with him.

I pulled my right hand away from my wrist and slid the blood soaked glove away.

'Wow, Dario said as we looked at my cut. That's pretty deep. You'll probably need stitches'.

'I don't know. I'm going to my truck Dario. I have all sorts of stuff down there, band aids and some antibiotic ointment.'

I moved my wrist around and looked closer at the deep gash.

'Okay Exi, I'll try to find Silvio.'

I wrapped my wrist with some paper towels and took the stairs down to my truck and gathered what I needed. I walked back up to the third floor where Dario and Silvio were waiting for me.

'What happened to you?' Silvio asked me as he saw me come into the room.

'I thought I was a goner for sure'.

I told him how the jagged ceramic toilet had slipped and cut me.

'Let me look at your arm', he said.

He wiped off the dried on blood, exposing the deep gash with a chunk of my inner flesh missing and a flap of skin left dangling, looking kind of like a partial eyelid.

'You might need stitches; you should maybe get two or three. You are lucky man, he said chuckling. The cut just missed that artery, see there?' he said pointing.

'Yeah, that was scary as hell. I've been through some tense situations in my life but that was different. I thought for sure I was going to join jackson and his clan and have to haunt the tower with them'.

They laughed.

'I'm feeling pretty weak so I'm going to take it easy for the rest of the afternoon if you don't mind. I'm just relieved that I pulled my arm back when I felt it cut me or I think it would have been worse'.

I had no doubt that any deeper and I might have bled to death right there on the sixth floor.

I used the antibiotic cream I had brought from the truck as well as a large band aid that Dario had found in the kit.

'Thanks a lot for helping me out. That could have been a lot worse'.

'No problem. Are you sure you don't want me to drive you to a clinic'?

'No, I'm okay boss; I'll just go up and sweep the seventh floor if that's okay and take it easy. It's almost quitting time anyway'.

'Sure but let me check your hand'.

He took my wrist and squeezed my fingers to see if my blood was flowing to my fingers.

'You see? You're fingers turn red right away so you did not cut an artery. Maybe jackson was protecting you; maybe you are lucky to be alive'.

'Never mind that Silvio, maybe jackson helped make it happen. I don't trust them any more than you do my friend'.

I went outside to my truck and had a quick cigarette then went up and finished the day taking my time sweeping on the seventh floor. I looked down at my wrapped up wrist and couldn't believe what had happened.

It seemed absurd to me. I pride myself on being safe at work. I'm constantly looking out that everyone else is safe as well.

I felt weak and dizzy. I worked at a slow pace and in my mind went through how the toilet could have slipped like that. The more I thought about it the more I believed the toilet had some help, like it was pushed but just slightly. It was similar to when I had fallen backwards from the ladder.

There were spirits in this building and I believed they were getting even more aggressive. My arm was sore. It was three thirty in the afternoon so I got my things from the window ledge and took the elevator down and drove home.

At home I carefully took a shower and looked at my wrist. It was gross. I thought of how everything that kept happening in the tower seemed to be getting more dangerous. All the stories we were hearing about past suicides, and the strange and intrusive things happening to us were unnerving.

I was noticing more faces and weird shapes in the videos that I was taking, and the 'accidents' really didn't seem like accidents at all.

I decided not to get stitches.

I poured some grappa (moonshine) on my cut. I hadn't yelled that loud in a long time. The alcohol cleaned my wrist out good preventing any infection from starting. Tina cooked up steak that evening. It was a good source of iron and protein after loosing all that blood.

'Here', she said, handing me a small wooden cross she had gotten from the holy land. It had a safety pin attached to it.

'This way you're protected from the front and back.'

'Thank you sweetheart, I don't know what I would do without you.'

She was my best friend and she understood how potentially dangerous the spirit world could be. I slept in the next morning from feeling so exhausted.

My arm felt tender and I kept it wrapped up. Before leaving for work I poured more moonshine on the cut and quietly yelled again while clenching my teeth.

Driving to work that day I thought of quitting the jobsite, again.

I felt oppressed and overwhelmed and questioned my sanity. But deep down I knew I didn't want to be defeated by this or give up or give in. I wanted to face my invisible fears and somehow they seemed to keep drawing me back.

1} feminine-voice 2} masculine-voice 3} masculine-voices 4} masculine-voice 5} masculine-voices 6} laughing, masculine-voice, laughing 7} masculine-voices 8} masculine-voice 9} masculine-voices 10} masculine-voice 11} masculine-voice 12} masculine-voice 13} masculine-voice 14}masculine-whisper.

Chapter Six; We Have More Tricks

1ˢᵗ Corinthians 5: 5 **To *deliver such a one unto Satan, for the destruction of the flesh, that the spirit may be saved in the day of the Lord Jesus.***

As the days rolled on, arriving at work felt more and more oppressive. Just looking at the monstrous tower gave me the eerie feeling that I was constantly being watched. Living in this vast world are spirit beings, invisible entities revealing themselves in different ways at different times. This old motel was definitely haunted. Everyone at work had been infected.

Ghosts' exposing themselves to me was a violation of my space, my peace of mind and my personal well being and safety. Most of the voices I had recorded so far were aggressive but intelligent. The recordings don't lie. I have them. It is what it is.

It amazed me how powerful and smart the spirits at the motel were. I realized I had to be stronger and smarter than they were. I was just hoping I would be able to do that. Being exposed to this haunting sharpened my own limited awareness of myself; what scared me and what didn't. I became more convinced that God knows what he is doing and that there's a reason for everything but it was just too vast for me at least to understand it. Sometimes we just have to go through the motions and walk in the strength and faith that we presently have, because life is always changing.

This haunting was a very personal thing to me. I believed I had been attacked. All the recorded evidence of voices, pictures and communication with these entities confirmed the reality of the insanity there. It seemed like the ghosts were part of an insane asylum setting.

It became part of a regular form of battle for me, after arriving in the parking lot in the mornings to reflect on my strategy plan at the Park Sets Motel. I didn't obsess about it but my spirit seemed to adjust to a different kind of reality. I was grateful for God's protection in that place. I just hoped that I deserved His mercy as well. There aren't too many guarantees that I have learned of in my short life. Survival I think is sometimes just like rolling dice and hoping for the best outcome.

On most mornings I was tired physically, but I always tried to focus on staying as mentally alert as possible. With a painted cross on my back and one hanging from my shirt pocket I felt somewhat secure. But at the same time maybe that was a magnet somehow attracting some of the spirits that were all around us. I did feel vulnerable but I certainly wasn't bored.

Being at work became a game to me. Some sort of game of survival; who could out last who, maybe who could out scare who more. Life is just a big game after all. And for the most part the crew just accepted the harassment. Maybe we tolerated each other as well. I wondered about that sometimes. The tension in the tower was thick which I believe at least contributed to the negativity we all felt and reacted to. And I believe the ghosts were upset and confused, maybe even scared in their own way with all the changes to their environment. And all the memories and the dramas over the years in the motel that they had witnessed or were involved in somehow, up until now at least were coming to an end. I would be upset too.

Not going down without a fight was something I kind of respected about these ghosts and I think they knew it. And I also hoped they knew I wasn't going to let them control me either. If they were here, I mean without a doubt really here they had just better leave me alone from now on or deal with the consequences is how I tended to think about it all. It was a learning experience for me in unfamiliar territory. Training day was every day and one day at a time.

I knew they were here, and from some of the recorded voices I had reviewed so far I believed they were aware that I knew they were real. I was on edge at times not knowing if a spirit was an inch away from me or around a corner, or taking a ride in the elevator with me. Some still photos I had taken show faces in and around all five of the elevators.

As I made my way to the third floor lunch room that morning, Silvio told me he wanted me to grab what tools I needed and a plastic cart and to work down in the basement. He wanted me to scrape down the peeling paint on the ceiling then tidy the room up. It was going to be our new change room and tool room while the third floor was being demolished.

I found what I needed and took the elevator to the main floor and wheeled a cart on wheels down the long hallways and into the men's old locker room change room, close to the indoor pool. I got myself organized and got ready to start.

More and more I was being sent to different floors to work alone. Being alone in this locker room was creepy but Silvio often asked me if I was okay working alone. I was and I had to be. I know he was dealing with the ghosts in his own way too and I knew I wasn't always really 'alone'.

'What do you say jackson?'

As I tried to motivate my body to start scraping the ceiling I sang some music that came to my mind.

I heard some low whistling as Silvio came around the corner into the room.

'You freaked me out', I said, as he chuckled and walked over.

'Its you that is jumpy'.

'You scared the hell out of me.'

He laughed for a while knowing I was spooked then he told me when he walks into a room so as not to scare one of us he will whistle or make some noise.

'I am glad that you do man I would be even more freaked out. It's alright. I won't be long anyway I'll get this room finished in no time'.

He showed me what he wanted done then picked up a few pieces of brass couplings from the floor then left down the long hall towards the main elevators.

I started by sweeping with the push broom clearing off the floor so I could walk safely. I found a fire hose that was stretched out into the room from its case in the hall that led to the discothèque. I wrapped it up so it was out of my way. I got goose bumps knowing the ghosts were around.

'Creepy, hoo, hoo, yeah baby.'

'Is there a ghost in here with me?'... 'So why are you here I wonder?'… 'A nice clean floor you've got it made now man'

After sweeping enough debris out of my way I took the large plastic shovel jackson, and started scraping the ceiling.

I had that strange feeling again like someone was watching me and as I faced the hallway to the washrooms and longer hallway to the night club I said;

'Get lost you guys'.

1} "GIVE UP"…

I moved around the room, scraping the ceiling

'Don't pick on me it's just my job. What can I say dude'?

I felt a presence around me and decided to recite some spiritual poetry I had learned.

'First I want to thank you Lord, for being who you are. For coming to the rescue of a man who's drifted far. For calling me to be your son, calling me to serve, Lord the way you bless my life is more than I deserve. This is my prayer; I lift it up to you, knowing you care even more than I do. This is my prayer lifted in your name, your will be done, I humbly pray. And keep us from the power that devours, amen'.

Just then I noticed something out of the corner of my eye.

'Ahhhhh!'.......

'Hey. How you doing? You scared me', I said, feeling embarrassed for yelling. An older man was standing in the doorway. He was about sixty years old.

'You think there is a ghost in this place?', he said.

'I don't think he will touch me', I said pointing to my cross. It can't sneak up on me at least', I added with a chuckle.

'There are lots of ghosts in here man', he said.

I recognized him as the maintenance man I had seen a number of times over the months. He worked for the motel.

'You think so? You have worked here a long time?' I asked him.

'A long time. There are lots of ghosts here, hundreds', he said.

'I think I have seen one'.

'One? You are lucky'.

'On Friday I saw a shadow on the fourth floor'.

'Yeah, there is more than one. They used to hide in the tower. When there was a fire, people died in the tower and it turned into a place where people would kill themselves and since then lots of people have killed themselves here over the years in all the different rooms'.

I don't know why this stranger was telling me all this but I was grateful that he was. Knowledge is power.

'Since I have been working here about thirty five people have killed themselves'.

'You have been working here a long time?'

'Since 1978'.

'Wow that's a long time. I guess you were here for the fire. What's your name?'

'Carey'.

'I'm Exi', I said as we shook hands.

'See, when a person rented a room that is their property for two days or three days. And they put a sign on their door to not be disturbed. And they pop a lot of pills or different things. It's when they are supposed to check out they notice they haven't checked out, that they go and open the door.'

'Who is it that goes and checks is it the front desk?'.

'Yes the front desk'.

'That must be very traumatic for someone to find bodies like that'.

'Oh they are used to it. That other motel that they tore down, one time a lady, she drank some sort of liquor and she jumped right through over the balcony and killed herself and she dropped in some bushes out there stone dead. Some they find dead some die in their rooms'.

'There was a woman working here as duty manager and I was working the weekend shift. She was a nice pretty woman a big woman and she had this old bloke giving her sex you know, he was naked as a jay bird and the old guy had a heart attack and died. By the time they got some oxygen to him he had turned blue. That happened on a Saturday night, and then I came back to work the following Monday'.

'I never saw that woman's face again. She was just up and gone'. He chuckled remembering the event.

'That's crazy', I said; 'So you see these ghosts sometimes over the years?'

'Well when I am working some place and they are used to me by now anyways right, they don't bother me; you are working in a room and you know there is something, another presence or another being beside me and you know sometimes you will smell something or hear something, like if I hear something drop and I just say that's okay, it's okay.' He chuckled then said; 'take it easy man'.

'I will Carey and you too. Good to meet you.' And he was gone.

Well that was interesting and kind of bizarre too I thought as I scraped more of the ceiling. I felt a little more relaxed after our talk.

If any ghoulies had been listening maybe they had followed their old friend Carey. That was fine with me. Deep down I knew the more they were away from me the better. It was draining being haunted. I rhymed off some more poetry as I worked.

2} "NO PROBLEMS".

'Cleaning this mess up for you dudes'

3} "THAT'S NO COMFORT".

4} "NICE BROOM".

I was getting the creepy feeling again that something was watching me. Oh well I thought. Not everyone gets to work in a haunted building. Lucky me.

'That's crazy, just crazy', I said as I thought about it again.

'Just cleaning up for you; respect. Gotta have respect. Respect, respect, respect. Alright, covered by the blood.'

I was almost finished down there and thank goodness because it was dungy in this part of the basement. One of the creepiest rooms I had ever been in. I couldn't wait to get out of there.

'Ooh yeah baby one more area to go and I'll be out of your way. I'll leave it nice and clean for you. Sorry for the noise I hope you have enjoyed my singing. Alright, I'm out of here good riddance and good night'

Arriving at work the next day I took my time and organized my things and put my work boots on. On the days I would show up early I took advantage of the time to relax and reflect on what was going on in my life, and in the world around me.

Mother's day had just passed. I thought of my dear mother and the nice weekend we had spent together. She would be eighty years old in July. Tina and I tried to see our folks as often as we could at least on a regular basis. My mother had a form of dementia so she wasn't aware that I was working in a haunted building. Knowing my mother she would have been amused.

Tina's mother had seen a few of the still photos I had taken and she laughed. She thought it was neat. Her father didn't want to hear about it. That type of thing scared him for some reason. It scared me too more and more as I found image after image on my digital camera and when it was all said and done I had recorded over one hundred voices from the other side. Some were whispers while some were clear voices, either answering questions or blurting out words and sentences to me or to each other.

After lunch I met up with Lucas in front of the elevators. We got into elevator three, the better of the two still working.

'So, he said; 'how did you enjoy being stuck in the elevator a while back. How long were you stuck again?'

'Almost an hour; it wasn't a whole lot of fun that is for sure'.

'I was stuck in it too back in January I think, yeah'.

'You were stuck in that other one too'?

'No this one we are in', he said.

'Wow, so how was that, what happened'?

'I don't know. I took it up to the top floor but it got stuck in between the twentieth and twenty first floors. Paco was up there waiting for me and we were the only ones in the building so he could hear me yelling for him'.

'You must have been freaked out, it's pretty creepy eh and you were way up there too, just hanging. That's what scares me for some reason; the thought of being stuck so high up and running out of air', I said.

'I didn't have to worry about running out of air. Paco was on the other side of the doors and he went and got a crow bar and pried the doors open. That took about an hour total'.

'So what you just climbed out then?'

'No, it wasn't that simple, yo. I was a little worried about climbing out and getting crushed if it started moving so it took me a while to decide to do it. I knew I had to. It was on the weekend so unless I called the fire dept it would have taken a while probably for someone on call to get here. Plus it was getting late in the day. Eventually I just decided to do it so I used my hands and climbed up onto the twenty first floor while Paco helped by pulling me out'.

'That's wild man. So how long were you in there'? I asked.

'For almost two hour's man! Climbing through there was a pretty scary feeling and you know I've done some wild things I'm not a big chicken but that was pretty intense. This freaking place is something else', he said as he got out onto the twenty third floor.

'See you man', I said as the doors closed.

This place was crazy and it was making us all uncomfortable. I believed that the experiences we had gone through came down to this; some of it could be explained and debunked, but a lot of it couldn't. Most of the time we kept our experiences to ourselves. I remembered Silvio telling me before they had laid off a worker named Reed, how he would catch him sticking his head into the openings in the walls and doors to look up and down the elevator shaft. He used a flashlight to look around to see if anything was there. We all seemed to be oppressed in one way or another.

That afternoon I went back to the third floor and took it easy. It was all light work for me getting rid of light debris in all the rooms so we could knock down the walls in the next few days. It was another interesting day as usual. I had gotten through the day without too much stress. I was pleased that I was being sent to work alone even though I was routinely intimidated by a spirit.

I woke up the next morning to a bright warm sun. Standing on the balcony enjoying my coffee I took some time for some serenity before starting my busy routine for the day. My peace of mind seemed to dissipate as I drove up the winding road to the big motel. I saw it as a matter of battle. I had no idea what the ghosts at the motel were going through but I knew some of them were malicious and spiteful. My guard always seemed to be up and I was ready for anything.

It would be another extremely hot day, just one of many that summer. I made my way around and asked anyone I saw if they wanted new gloves. I noticed someone in the back elevator shaft room standing in front of the elevator doors near the edge of a small pile of cinder block rubble. I asked him if he needed gloves from the doorway of the room. It was near pitch black in the room as the sun would not shine its fading rays onto this side of the tower until much later in the day. He reached out to take the gloves from me, not taking his eyes off of the partially opened doors of the elevator shaft, looking mesmerized as if he was feeling uncomfortable for some reason. I just remember the look of puzzlement on his face like he was trying to figure something out, a bit apprehensive about something. He had either seen something or heard voices coming from the shaft.

I felt bad for all of us that way; for us humans having to work in that haunted environment, and for the spirits for having their temporary homes invaded.

I believe human beings have authority over ghosts. If I had to or needed to I would try to remember that fact. It also helped me to deal with my own fear of knowing we were rubbing shoulders with the other side.

From the recorded proof I had so far nothing would surprise me. It might scare me but it wouldn't surprise me.

I walked up to the sixth floor. After filming in through a hole in some blocks at the back service elevator wall, I filmed the corner of the back room.

'This is the sixth floor', I said as I scoped the room.

5} "CLEAN IT UP".

Monday morning came too soon. Over the next few weeks I found myself more and more intrigued with the voices and still photos I was getting from the motel. I was hoping that the ghosts would talk even more to hopefully help me gain more insight into what was going on in there and why.

I was working alone more each day now out of hearing range of the other workers in the building. We rarely saw the bosses either as most of the salvageable leftovers were gone.

One video I shot was of the back elevators. One of the doors was partially opened exposing the blackness of the shaft. A thick piece of plywood was blocking the opening for safety with the word 'Danger' painted on it in red. A pile of block rubble once a wall forming part of the laundry chute had been knocked down and would be cleaned up later.

I focused the video into the darkness hoping to see something after reviewing it later. Catching an image would turn out to be hit or miss at any time in the motel maybe depending on what the spirits were up to on any given day. When and where they would haunt us was always different and unpredictable. They seemed to have a pattern of staying out of sight and not being visible to any of us. They seemed to prefer it that way even though they knew we were aware of them. They proved that many times with the things they said and in response to questions asked of them.

The spirits heard me talking and understood what I was saying. That I didn't doubt at all. They too can be manipulative and if they choose to scare you they will try to whatever way that they can.

The next video I wanted to take was of the purple striped stairwell. By now I knew the layout of the tower and took the outside entranceway that led back up the tower via the stairs. I remember being apprehensive as I reached the start of the stairwell from the ground floor. I turned on the video and made my way up the partially lit up staircase. As I reached the double floor section past the second floor entrance, it turned to pure black with that light burnt out until I reached the next landing. I was nervous doing this and could tell that my heart was beating just a little faster than usual. I knew some people had died in here but I was determined to face my fear of it. I made my way through the momentary blackness and climbed the stairs to the fifth floor. I moved the camera slowly to look around the stairwell from the landing and then slowly walked down to the third floor landing.

I found the glass part of a red exit sign that used to hang on the ceiling in front of the doorway and displayed it to the camera then filmed the stairs behind me...

6} "F*#K THAT"...

I left my camera to record while I walked around the floor to get a better idea of how much was left to do.

7} "GIVE UP"...

8} ……. "DIFFICULT".

I later went back to retrieve the camera. I picked it up and moved it around the elevator room and asked;

'You guys in here'?

I turned around and filmed the room facing the doorway.

It had a Gideon bible hanging from a wire on the ceiling. I guess someone had hung it there as a form of protection. Good idea. I made my way to the elevators and filmed the front foyer then headed home for the night.

I usually operated the elevators. It worried me at times working the elevator having been stuck and all. But both elevators were working and I always carried my cell phone so I hoped I'd be alright. It also gave me more freedom to film more of the building and I was grateful for that.

I was left by myself and on one of my lunch breaks one week I ventured up the purple stairwell climbing slowly and steadily to each landing.

At the twenty sixth floor landing I noticed that the stairs continued up so I nervously walked up into pitch blackness again at a section without any light. I hung on to the railing and went to the landing then turned and noticed the next landing with a sliver of daylight shining through the steel door leading to the roof of the tower. I videoed to my right and noticed a room, an electrical room.

I climbed the last few stairs and walked through the doorway filming to my right.

9} "SWEETIE'S INSIDE"…

It was a typical room crammed with pipes, duct work and vents that at one time helped keep the building functioning. I turned into the dark and tried to open the roof door.

10} "I PUKED TODAY".

It wouldn't open. It was locked. I carefully made my way down the darkened stairwell and entered the twenty fifth floor filming two more mechanical rooms. I tried another door to the roof but it was also locked.

I walked back onto the main floor...

11} "YOU MAKE ME FEEL BAD"...

and then made my way around and said;

'I command you in Jesus' name. I want you to appear.... You don't have to be afraid of me. Let me know you's are here...... Come on. Don't be afraid'.

I walked into a side ventilation room about six by twelve feet in size. The ceiling and the walls half way up were covered in thick black soot. The now missing generator must have been put to the test.

'I'm sorry you guys got hurt. I really am.'

I kept walking around to my left and entered another mechanical room.

'You guy's here? Come out', I said, then turned left into a short hallway to the grey striped stairwell. It had a flight of stairs leading up to another roof door and mechanical or boiler room. I videoed the area and checked the door which was locked then I went back down and took a walk back through the twenty fifth floor.

'Let me know you're in here come on out'.

'Come out, come out wherever you are. I know you guys are here', I said as I made my way to the purple striped stairwell on the twenty third floor.

I filmed the stairwell then slowly turned to walk zooming the camera to view out, walking slowly past the rooms.

I went to a window and filmed the view. I turned and walked towards the elevators.

The next morning I was back up on the twenty third floor. I felt drawn to it somehow sensing spirit activity there so I did more recording.

'Hey you guys, jackson or whoever else is up here. We're pretty much finished if you guys are up here come and say hello'.

I paused … 'Why are you here? …. Well say something or do something. Let me know you are here'.

I paused again.

'Show yourself wherever you are…. Come on out. Don't be afraid. What's happening'? I said as I walked to a full barrow.

'Smoke damage everywhere.'

I zoomed in to film different patches of black soot left by the terrible fire from years back. It was scattered throughout the building.

'I like you guys especially jackson….. Come on out and let me know what's going on'

It was great to be getting all the recordings. Yesterday I was on the twenty second floor and this morning I would be working on the twenty first floor. Hopefully I could film the building from the top down before the work ran out. At least that is what I hoped. I was going to try.

I began on the twenty fourth floor. I could just imagine people sitting there years ago in the late evening enjoying a drink and maybe a cigar, chatting away enjoying their stay at the once posh and expensive motel.

I turned to my right to continue filming.

'It's a beautiful day… I'm sorry you's went through hell in this place…Maybe you guys should leave, you know? But come out and say hello. Don't be afraid.'

I walked back to the elevators.

I started working enjoying the peace and quiet of working alone, cleaning up and being able to take my time with the much lighter work. I remember how great it felt to rest my body, to not have to push it to the limit everyday like I had to at the start.

It was June already and we had been here almost four months. That was two months longer than it was suppose to last, but it was only a matter of time.

At lunch time I pressed the elevator button. I waited and waited but they must have been on service for the other workers so I decided that taking the stairs down twenty four floors wasn't so bad. It was much better than taking them up. It was also another opportunity to take more videos.

'Okay, I can't get the elevator so I'll walk down these stairs. If you demons want to pop up go for it' I said, as I started down the purple striped stairwell.

'Cause I would love to meet you in Jesus' name. Show yourself, say something or do something because I know you are around.'

As I reached the eighteenth floor I said; 'I know a bunch of you died on the stairwells here... Lots of noises pardon the interruptions... There are a couple of girls here too right? What do you's want.... Is there anything I can do to help just let me know.... Here we go'. [I was feeling pretty nervous at this point]

'One of you died here on the fourteenth floor. That Spanish man... Show yourself'.

As I reached the ninth floor I shut off the camera and hurried down the stairs to my truck, then drove to get a coffee.

It was interesting trying to communicate with the spirits. I was able to review and stay caught up with all the voices and still pictures I had recorded over the months.

It was crazy. I had the proof that they were here and they regularly tried to scare the heck out of me whether I knew it or not and it seemed that they just tried to make sure that we felt uncomfortable.

As I ate my lunch I relaxed under a tree in the shade letting the serene quiet help dissipate some of my spiritual stress. It was a beautiful blue sky with big puffy clouds. After lunch I took the elevator to the twenty fifth floor.

I walked the floor to my left, to the elevator shaft room.

'Not a very beautiful room', I said as I zoomed in on the smoke damage.

I made my way to the purple striped stairwell.

I had reviewed some video from yesterday and realized it had captured some human looking faces in the corner just inside the doorway.

I stayed on the landing just below knowing it was the same angle that I filmed yesterday. I was a little freaked out being up there as it was.

I figured the same theory as the white shadow image from the 24th floor could apply here. If there are no faces in today's video then yesterday something could have been staring at me from around the door frame.

I took the footage I wanted and headed down the stairs…

12} "THIS IS HOW WE LOOK"…

I stepped onto the twenty fifth floor.

I walked around to my left as I had done yesterday. I had to debunk something. My video from yesterday also showed what looked like a shrunken head sitting on a heater vent just inside the electrical room doorway. I walked through the short hall to the grey striped stairwell and slowly walked up to the landing, turning to face the stairs into the dark room. I walked up slowly, concentrating on the possible shrunken head. As I got closer I could see that it was a fire extinguisher hung up on the wall beside the heater. With just the top visible in the dim light it did look like some shrunken head, or something too weird.

'Not a ghost just a fire extinguisher', I said feeling relieved. These videos captured everything about this place in one way or another; the good the bad and the grotesque. I couldn't wait to find out if I had videoed the same faces again or not.

At home I reviewed the footage of getting to the doorway of the mechanical room. I slowed the video down. I looked at it a number of times and didn't notice any faces that I had filmed yesterday in the exact same spot.

Then I put the two video pictures side by side. The one from yesterday had a number of faces moving around. The second video was just the door frame. That really numbed my spirit. It was unbelievable. I was looking at the proof right in front of me.

This was exciting to me and intimidating at the same time. It was more and more overwhelming as I was finding all the faces and voices. I tried to reflect and had a few drinks out on my balcony, drinking slowly and taking everything in, trying to stay focused for the days ahead and willing the fear from my mind when it tried to bring me down.

I could literally feel the ghosts or demons around me. The ghosts were scaring everyone in the building. Little did I know I would need all the faith and courage I could find to stay in control in the old haunted tower.

1} masculine-whisper 2} masculine-voice 3} masculine-voices 4} masculine-voice 5} feminine-whisper 6} masculine-high-voice 7} masculine-whisper 8} masculine-deep-voice 9} masculine-voice 10} masculine-voice 11} masculine-whisper 12} masculine-whisper

I named her sweetie. She looks sweet enough though maybe looks are deceiving.

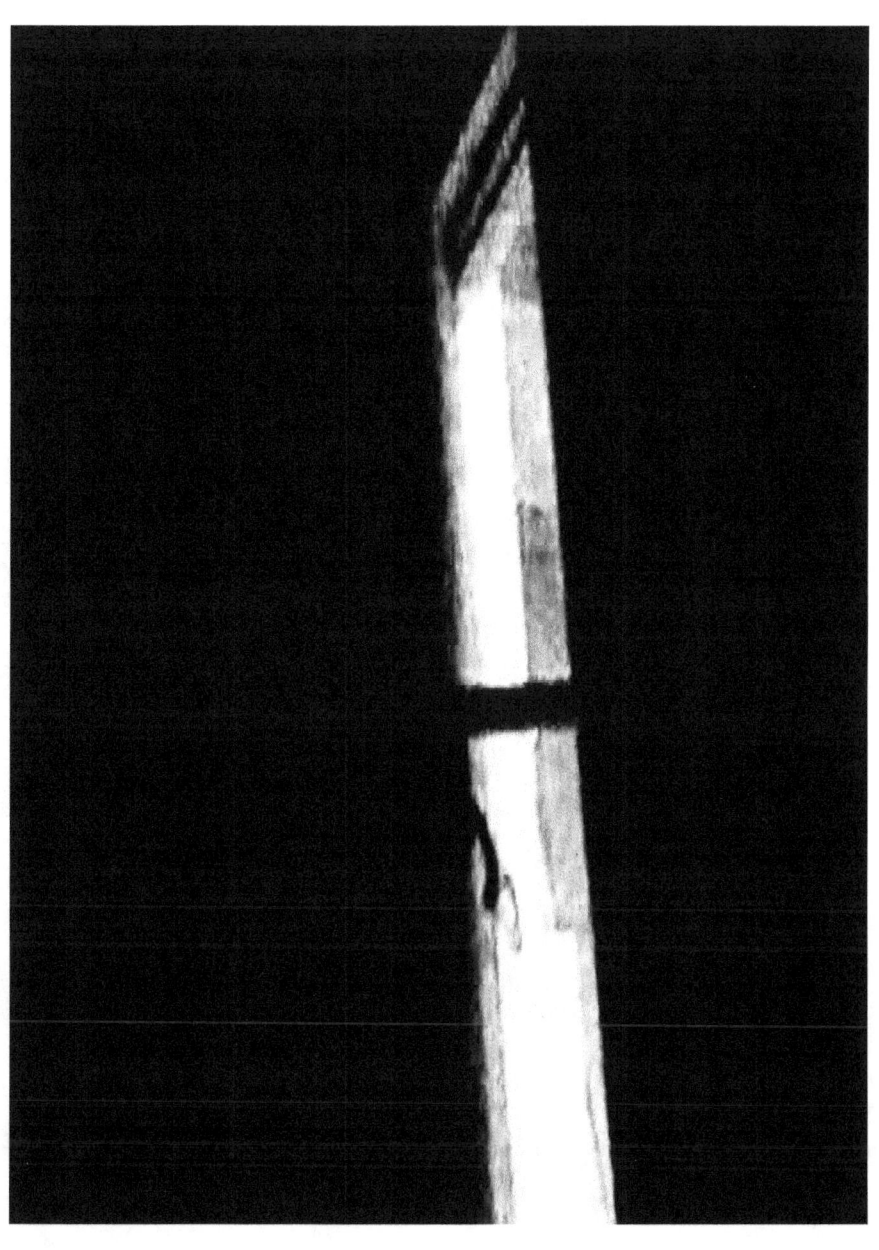

An old native spirit maybe.

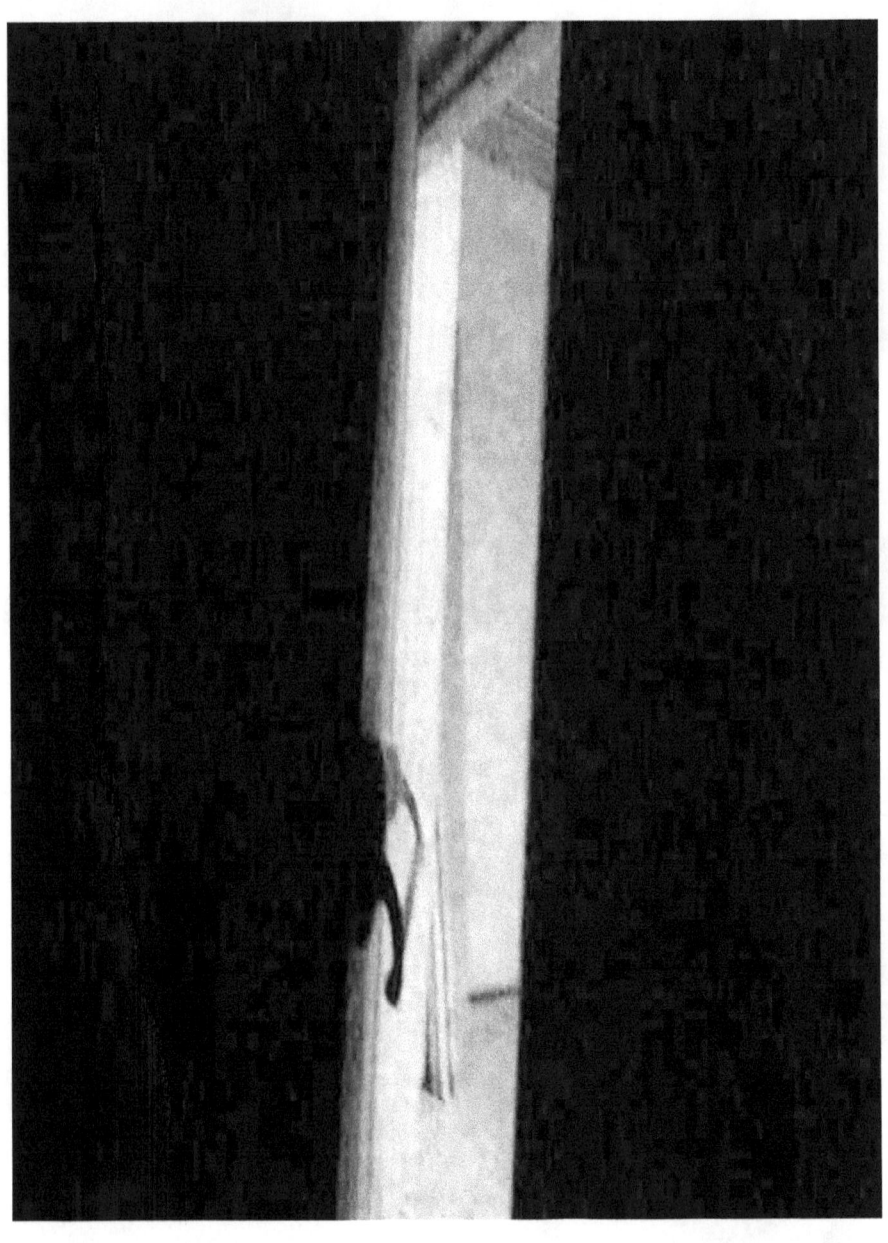

Photo of same area. Sweetie and her friends were no longer there.

I see a masked man in this photo (near the top center of the black hole) with two black eyes or wearing a mask. Looks like a couple of the spirits are hanging out in there. (side wall of one of the back service elevator rooms).

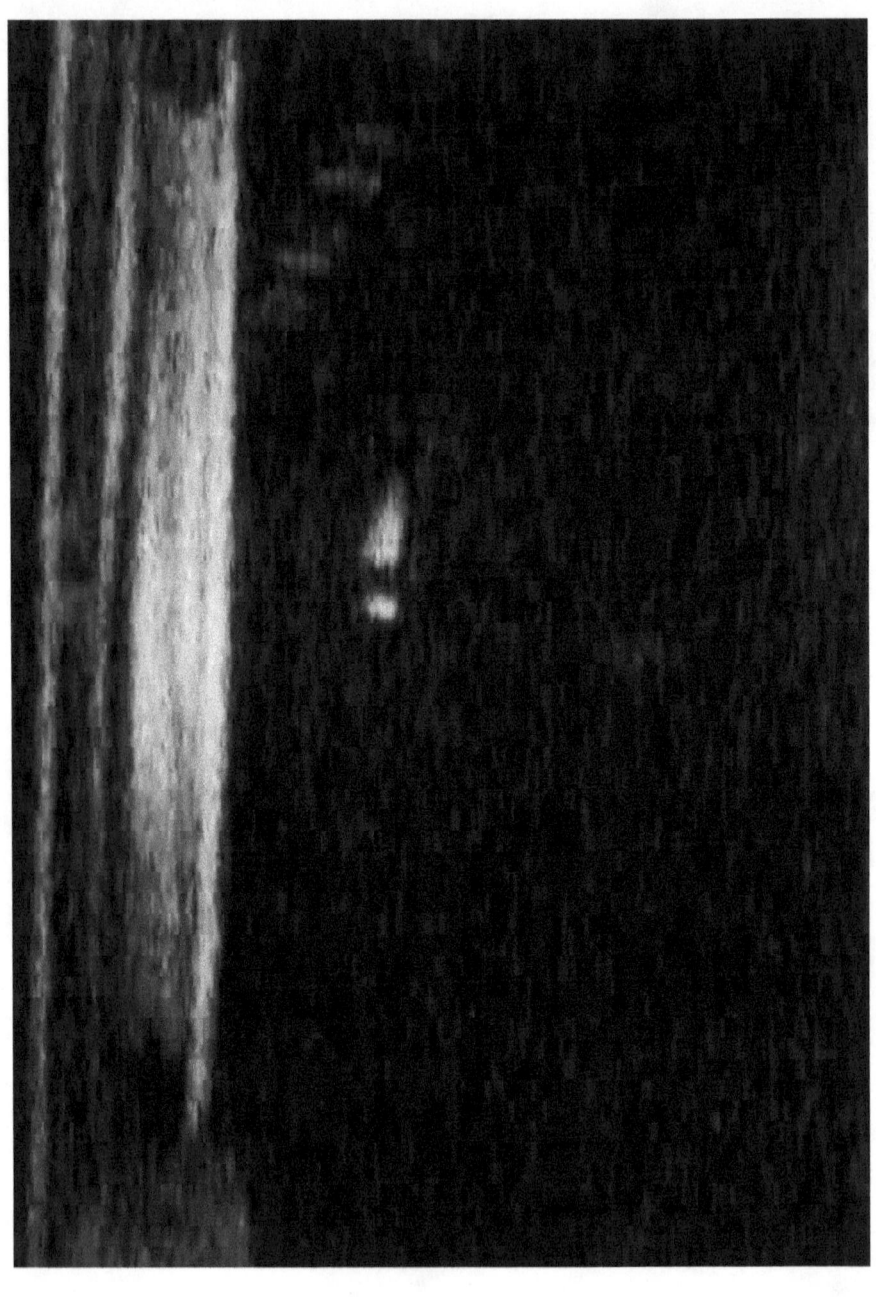

Casper the friendly ghost?™ (passenger elevator #3, looking down the shaft)

The Holy Bible we saved from one of the rooms. Someone hung it in mid air so the demons could see it.

Chapter Seven; We Lived In Heaven

Luke 8: 30 *And Jesus asked him, saying, What is thy name? And he said legion: because many devils were entered into him.*

My weekend started by sleeping in until nine a. m. knowing I wouldn't have to rush off to work.

It was mid June and the weather was sweet with the sun shining, the birds chirping and nature getting greener by the day.

I was feeling physically exhausted but content. I was grateful to be busy and productive. I was thankful I wasn't working as hard at the motel lately. My weekends were always my retreat away from the haunted building. It was like knowing you had to go to school Monday morning with the school bully always near by. The fight or flight response.

The weekend came and went like most of them, too quickly. Returning to work on Monday morning my brothers and I were informed by Silvio that half of the remaining crew would be laid off in the next few weeks.

So that was that, but first things first. What I thought of doing this morning for some reason was go up to the top floor in the purple striped stairwell and say goodbye to the ghosts I had videoed. According to Carey's observations they often hung out up there. That's where some of them were hanging out when I filmed them last week. I arranged to call Tina at work from my cell phone so she could hear me talking to them and besides, I was nervous about it so I wanted her on the phone in case anything happened. A man is only as brave as he gets over his fears.

I was disappointed about the up coming inevitable lay off. I hadn't had the chance to record as much of the building as I had wanted, to do more e.v.p. work. I knew the activity with the spirits had increased so I hoped I'd be one of the last to go.

I made my way up at break time and called Tina when I was ready to record.

'Hey sweetheart how are you... Yeah I'm up here I just have to get my recorder going..... Okay I'm climbing the stairs; 'hey guys, just me again..... I just wanted to say good bye, I wanted to say good bye to all you guys... And wanted to say...

1} "GO FOR IT"...

that I probably won't be here much longer', I said as I turned and walked back down the stairs.

'Yeah it's taping', I told Tina...... 'Well I had better let you go have a good day love ya, ciao'.

Silvio had been walking around on the floors during the morning and I didn't want him catching me talking to the elusive ghosts.

During the afternoon I did more e.v.p. work, working my way down starting on the twentieth floor.

'So what do you think of the renovations... Looks pretty good eh?....

You guys out here... My sweetie here?...

2} "OH, YES"...

'Jackson.'

I walked over to one of the windows and videoed the skyline.

'Downtown, and there's uptown'.

I took the elevator down one floor at a time and continued recording.

I walked to the stairwell landing; 'The death stairwell, the purple striped stairwell.'...

Next I went to sixteen then fifteen.

I stayed quiet while recording to give the spirits time they might need to process questions and blurt out anything verbal.

The smoke damaged stained concrete was more evident now, scattered here and there once hidden by the now smashed up cinder block walls. The black soot was thicker on the lower floors.

The next floor was the twelfth. It was one of the floors that felt more oppressive than some of the others. 'This is the twelfth floor.... Lots of pipes here for me to pick up'. I did my usual routine and filmed all the way around the floor, stopping to film the two sets of stairs and the back shaft rooms as I went along.

'This is where someone is supposed to have died', I said as I filmed the area; 'between the twelfth and fourteenth floors, right in here. You in here'? I said nervously...

3} "THAT'S WEIRD".... "LET'S HIDE"…….. "WHAT'S HE HIDING?"

After lunch I went back to the stale air on the twelfth floor. I turned on the camera and walked to my left to the purple striped stairwell, then the back elevator room.

'You're in here somewhere'.

Before I went home that day I took a longer video of the twelfth floor. I let it run while I took a short break. It wasn't as hot inside the tower today as it was humid and it felt great to cool off by the open window.

4} "REACH OUT TO ME"...

I finished a cigarette and left for the evening.

The next morning I started on the 25th floor. 'So what are you savages up to this weekend'... Its been a long week; we've been making a lot of noise. Sorry.... What do you guys think of the renovations eh'?

I was on an upper floor gathering plywood for the openings in the floors and just letting the recorder run.

5} "GLASS HURTS ME"…

'I hope we didn't make too much noise heh it's pretty noisy. I know you guys like coming up here… So my apologies and all that…....If you want to show yourself feel free. It doesn't bother me; I'm not going to hurt you… You guys have something to say to me, say it. I want to hear you's talking to me…. You are the lonely one's right?... Me too some times......You guys are tripping me out and it's been a real experience… I appreciate it…… Not everybody realizes and knows for sure that there are spirits around them. Thank you very much……What do you guys have to say about that… Speak up'….

6} "GOT THE PLAN"….

'Sorry for swearing. I've done a little bit of that in this place…… I cut myself again today; I hope you didn't help that happen did you?..... Why did you do that?...

7} "ACT YOUR AGE"….. "CAN'T HELP IT"…….. "URGH".

'Trying to hurt me?'….

It was a beautiful June morning as I drove to work that Friday.

I made my way up with my recorder and started my dialogue with them.

'So you guys. June 11th. You guys have anything you want to say, do it man say it man…. There was a nice smelling ghost in here I think it was Monday morning and wow, you blew me away baby… Is there something you want to say'?.... Sweet perfume mm, mm, mm.….Very nice thank you'….

8} "LISTEN"…………. "LISTEN".

I took the elevator up with Silvio to the 25th floor. He wanted me to gather up any debris on the 26th floor and then sweep it up.

'I guess I will sweep, take it easy and talk to the ghosts'.

When he left I resumed recording.

'Alright, I'm up here sweeping'.

The 26th floor had a hole in the concrete where some stairs had once been leading down to the 25th floor. It was covered over with some doors and thicker plywood. I knew Silvio was beneath me as I could hear him shuffling around.

I quietly slid a door away so I could crouch down and whisper;

'What are you doing down there'?

He looked up and saw me as I laughed.

'Did that scare you?'…

'No, not really', he said.

'I'm going to have to think of something else then'.

I continued sweeping thankful to be working with Silvio. The week was almost over. I covered the hole and continued talking while sweeping the floor.

'I scared him good jackson, what do you guys think was that scary or what?... Hey I'll tell you I was telling Silvio if I died and God sent me back for whatever reason, I'd maybe come back here with you guys if you would let me…. Would you let me?...... How about you sweetie?...... You would let me wouldn't you?.... Oh yeah sweetie and why not?'

I knew no one could hear me except the ghosts and it always gave me an uneasy feeling to sweep out the two stairwells especially the purple striped one.

'Hey sorry to interrupt you guys. Is it okay if I clean up? Just going to check this out….. Sorry, sorry dudes…. I know, I'll get out; it's not very nice of me…..No disrespect intended. Here I'll even close the door…. Have a good evening'.

I felt safer with the door closed, not that it made a lot of sense. They're ghosts after all. I would assume they could walk through a wall if they wanted to.

I walked over to the small window to check out the view.

'I'm gonna be gone in about a week.…. Its been a, its been an experience.….. I like you guys. Do you guys like me.… Not all of you's right? … I can sense it.…. Which one of you doesn't like me.… How come you don't like me, tell me.… Don't be scared …. I'm working at not being scared of you guys so, don't be afraid to tell me.… You know what I mean?'… With all due respect you're pretty rude if you're not talking to me'.

I gathered some bigger debris and attempted to finish cleaning up before quitting time.

9} "STEAL THE PIPES".

'Yeah I don't blame you guys for hanging out up here that's for sure. It's kind of cool.… You guys feel comfortable up here?.…. You guys talk as much as you want cause I'll be gone pretty soon so.… Here's your chance.…

'Here's your chance for some romance the girl with the smelly perfume dance'.….

I thought of some rhetoric as I worked.

'Nice smelling perfume is what my secret lady wore.… I think they call her incubus, or succubus or something to that report.… But she could be an ugly hag like the one in the movie The Shining™… Who tricks Jack Nicholson into thinking she's a beautiful brunette in the bathtub but she's just an old hag, a wolf in sheep's clothing'.

'I'll call you my sweetie.……. Are you the girl I saw on the wall in the video? Yeah? Beautiful. Beautiful honey, nice perfume.… I'd like to smell that perfume now. Come close to me sunshine and whisper sweet nothings in my ear.… Mm, mm, mm'.

10} "HAVE TO GO POOH" .…… "THERE'S THE PILE" … "URGH".

I swept up and made sure I did a good job hoping I wouldn't have to come up here again. Maybe I was making them angry in taunting them. I was pushing it, but deep down I wasn't afraid of them yet at the same time I kept my guard up. It's a strange reality that's hard to describe unless your part of a haunting.

I checked my watch and noticed the work week was finally over.

Monday morning I was on the twenty sixth floor once again. Right away I noticed the strong smell of alcohol. I looked everywhere on the floors and even checked the walls, but found no stains, bottles or containers. First the perfume now an alcohol odor. Would I have to work around smelly drunken demons?

'Well good morning everybody….. How was your weekend….. Is everybody good?…. Good, good, good…. It is Monday, June fourteenth already'…..

11} "NO POINT NOW"….

'I'm on the twenty sixth floor with my buddies and my honey…. How's my sweetie today?'

'Are you here are you with me?... Alright'………

12} "TAKE ME HOME"…….

'My sunshine how are you?..... My honey. What do you like better sunshine or sweetie?'

I knew from the evidence I had gathered that these ghosts were strange and they probably thought I was too, so I gave it my best shot to keep communicating.

'They did the mash; they did the monster mash, the monster mash, it was a grave yard smash, the monster mash…..Caught on in a flash, the monster mash…. They did the monster mash da ooh'…… 'I thought you guys would like that one', I said as I set a wheelbarrow down. I walked while whistling and then stopped for a break.

'Everybody still sleeping'….

13} "TWELVE DEMONS"…..

'Who's all here?....jackson are you around?.... Boring, boring, boring'…

I packed up what I needed and went to the twenty fifth floor.

'On the twenty fifth floor…. What are some of your names?..... My name is Exi and my wife's name is Tina, which I'm sure you're aware of. She is a demon warrior…… So if any of you are demons, which I'm sure some of you are, be nice or I'll send my wife after you…….. She's a little concerned about you and me sweetie….. Kind of funny eh hoo, hoo, hoo'.

'I can see clearly now the rain is gone'. This song is for you sunshine, sweetie;

'I can see all obstacles in my way…. Gone are the cloudy skies that blinded me….. It's gonna be a bright, bright, sun shiny day……. Do, do, do, do, do it's a blue sky. I can see all obstacles in my way. This song is for sunshine, sweetie and succubus; 'It's gonna be a bright, bright, sunshiny day. Yeah a sun shiny day.'

14} "THERE'S LUNCH"

Singing to the ghosts helped with the anxiety of being there. If they kept responding it was worth the effort.

I walked around and rummaged through some leftovers in the piles that I could salvage as mementos from this unique concrete tower, put some things in a plastic bag and buzzed for the elevator to go down for break. It was another hot day with the humidex at around thirty four degrees.

I sat in my truck, grateful once again for the air conditioning and my wonderful wife's cooking. I looked at all the mementos in the cab of the truck I had taken from the motel. It was piling up. I grabbed the camera and some Gatorade™ then made my way back up the stairs. I took the grey striped stairwell up to twenty six. I had been up there in the morning and noticed the door to the roof was open. It led to the lower part of the roof with a small walkway surrounding a massive sized compressor. I turned on the camera to video.

'This is the twenty sixth floor it's beautiful up here', I said as I viewed the awesome scenery of the parks greenery from so high up. 'The big blue sky'.

15} "YOU NEED TO GET THE LADDER IF YOU CAN"…

I videoed the massive steel compressor and walked around to the back of the unit, pointing the camera up to the clear sky above the twelve foot wall.

16} "I CAN KILL"…

On the roof area I took another short video, this time taking footage through the cut out concrete openings facing the outer wall which exposed the picturesque wide open greenery ….

17} "TOUCH THOSE TREES"…

I viewed the different angles of the scenery then went back to twenty five and took the elevator to the sixteenth floor.

I turned on the video camera facing it across the room to the purple striped stairwell entrance. I focused on this area for a minute letting the camera run…

18} "COME…. HERE"…

I moved the camera around and took some video of the now grey cloudy sky line then walked to my left filming the fire hose cabinet.

19} "WHO'S THERE"?

'Jackson and his five brothers eh?....Where art thou Pontiac,™ I said as I scanned the floor with the video first to my left then my right, filming the back room through the doorway entrance.

The next day after having my lunch in the comfort of my vehicle I took my audio recorder with me for the afternoon. I made my way up to my work floor and started to record.

'Well that was a darned good lunch….What do you guy's have to say?.... Hey I have some questions. Do you guys sleep in the daytime or night time?.....Or whenever you want?...... Daytime say yes…… Night time say yes……When ever you want?...... Cool. Cool!.... Alright', I said as I rolled a cart on wheels to a pile of debris and spent some time placing the heavy metal into the cart.

20} "DROP THAT".

I tried to think of things to say that would make any sense but it was harder to do than I thought. The voices that I was recording didn't make much sense either.

'If you guys have something to say why don't you just say it….. Do you like me?'…..

'Do you's hate me?'……

21} "YES"…… "HA, HA, HA, HA, HA, HA"……...

On Wednesday morning I went to floor fifteen to finish carting the debris to bring down stairs.

'How are you today sweetie? Are you okay?…… Cleaning up real nice for you's…… Doing a good enough job or what?'….

22} "NO"….

I swatted the dust from my gloves.

I struggled to lift part of a steel door frame into the cart and said; 'Another fine predicament you've '….

23} "GOTTEN ME INTO".

In hind sight I believe at this point in time something sinister was happening to my soul.

'The boss is here today so behave', I told the silent air.

'How's my sweetie this morning'….. 'My wife is jealous of you'……. I smelled you. I smelled the perfume'….

I rummaged through a pile of debris in a room and found an old newspaper cartoon section and read;

'Keeping up with current events in the lives of Charlie Brown™ and the peanuts gang. Alright, wa, wa, wa, wa.'….

24} "YOU'RE MINE"….

I went to the different piles and separated the metal from the dirt….

25} "WHERE'S IT AT?"…

"IT'S IN HIS SHIRT, CAN'T REACH"…………..

"THAT'S OKAY"…

I was at the back rooms and knew I wasn't alone.

'Good morning' I said, to try to help rid myself of the temporary fear.

I rolled an empty wheelbarrow to another pile…

26} "GIVE UP PUNK AND FIGHT, AGAINST THE WIZARDS"…

I picked the metal out and went to the next one…

27} "GO UP AND DOWN STAIRS, GO RUN THEM"…

Thursday morning I resumed my daily ritual and kept alternating between audio and video. I started by taking a video on the twenty fifth floor. It was a beautiful bright sunny morning as I psyched myself out for another weird day. As I reviewed more and more recordings I realized just how haunted the building was and now I was getting my way working alone, on the twenty fifth floor. Silvio sent me up there to clean up what was left of an eight by twelve foot wall that he had smashed apart the day before.

I started the video outside on one of the balconies. It was a crisp beautiful morning. 'Twenty fifth floor, Thursday June seventeenth'.

I zoomed in to get closer to a part of the park across the street; 'And here's a picture of a spooky little spot where they might have held rituals of some sort, I don't know.'

It was a group of picnic tables in a circle.

28} "TURN AROUND… RUN"…

'A beautiful shot of the city', I said as I scoped out the scene. 'And there's a great big eagle around here some where and of course lots of ghoulies'. I turned and walked back to film the demolished wall.

'And here's the purple striped stairwell, back elevator shaft, all the rubble.'

29} "I LEARNED THE WAY HOME"…

'It was either a falcon or eagle a big brown one', I said, as I thought of the large bird Silvio and I had seen fly onto the balcony first thing in the morning.

It had startled us and I couldn't believe that I had seen such a majestic creature so close up. As soon as it noticed us in the hallway it squawked, flapped its enormous wings and flew off.

'I pray in Jesus' name to see it again.'

If only I could get some pictures or video of it, that would be a bonus for sure. I started cleaning the mounds of blocks.

30} "STOP"… (feminine voice)… "I'VE HAD ENOUGH"…

"F*#K HIM"…

I placed a few more blocks in and sang a rendition of an old country song I had learned as a teenager called 'After Sweet Memories'.

As I slid the barrow out of my way a police siren was going off in the distance.

31} "HE'S IN TROUBLE"… "I DON'T CARE".

I picked up the bigger pieces of block then started shoveling the rest.

I filled the first barrow moved it away and started filling the second.

32} "PRAY FOR ME"…

I filled the second one and moved it too…

33} "WHERE'S HIS HAT?"

I filled the third one and moved the camera for a different angle then sang another song.

'Sunshine on my shoulders makes me happy'. [Voice in the background; 'yeah ooohh oooohhh,'] I put a block in; ['yoooouuu']

I saw something out of the corner of my eye, off to my left and took an automatic fighting stance as I yelled;

'Aaaaaahhhhhhh'.

As I walked around a corner I noticed Silvio. 'You bad man', I said as he approached me, laughing heartily. I guess that's what I got for trying to scare him not so long ago.

'You scared the shit out of me man', I said.

'No! Really?, he said as he continued laughing. Really? I thought you were not afraid to work alone.'

'Well no I'm not really. Just when you sneak up on me', I said. If he only knew the real reasons why, I wondered how he would handle it.

The next day I recorded for more e.v.p. 'Morning, morning, morning', I said, greeting the invisible world.

'Sorry for the noise. You know how it is. How many of you are there in here would you's please tell me?..... More than ten?.... More than twenty?.... More than fifty?.... Just tell me yes or no.... More than fifty?....... Thanks.'

I took a short break to cool off as it was extremely humid already though it was only eight thirty in the morning.

34} "DON'T YOU LAUGH AT ME".....

I swept the hallway awhile then continued at the purple striped stairwell entrance.

'You in here? I heard somebody died in here. I'm sorry.'

I picked up any small metal I found mixed in with the piles of debris in the rooms making my way around dropping a few pieces as I worked. I noticed a quarter on the floor and dropped it as I tried to pick it up…

35} "CALL IT", "IT'S HEADS"…

I rolled a small cart around with me collecting the metal until break time.

After the morning break I took the elevator to the eleventh floor.

'Eleventh floor. How are you today spirit on the eleventh or twelfth floor?…. Doing alright?…….. How about I just clean it all nice for ya?…. If you don't mind…. Thank you, thank you very much'.

36} "GET OUT YOU ANIMAL".

'You want a piece of granola bar?, I asked as I ate one. 'You guys eat food or what?'

I finished eating, getting some needed energy and water then cooled off by the open window.

37} "WE'RE IN HELL".

I finished my break to the noise of Papa hammering away at a wall some floors down from me.

My work day was going smoothly as I separated material into separate piles on the eleventh floor.

38} "GO"… "NO"…

I felt that a presence was near me.

I tried my best to ignore the way they made me feel but my spirit was aware of it so I couldn't.

I eventually took the number three elevator to the ninth floor. The doors started opening, then stopped. There was about a foot of space in the elevator doorway. I could see the ninth floor and wished I was on it. Then the doors closed.

If I got out I vowed I'd never take the elevators again.

At least I had my cell phone. I thought of pressing the door open button but nothing happened. I pried the doors and tried to push them open. It was like a movie. They would barely open. I pressed door open button again but the doors remained closed. Then just as quick they opened up and I hurried out onto the ninth floor.

I stared at the elevator like an enemy who had tried to hurt me. It started buzzing as it slowly closed. It opened up again so I reached inside and pressed the main floor button. It buzzed again as it closed briefly then opened quickly starting to beep again as it got ready to close. When it opened again I reached inside and flicked the service button to on than off to see if that would fix it. It just kept beeping and opening and closing on its own. It was bizarre.

I wasn't looking forward to climbing the stairs from now on but that's what I would do. There was no way I was getting stuck again. Too many deadly scenarios ran through my head. It was one thing to be stuck in a modern day elevator but getting stuck in these elevators wasn't a good scene at all.

I called Silvio from my cell to let him know what the elevator was doing. I waited for him on the ninth floor. He came up to the ninth in the centre elevator and eventually got in the elevator and managed to get it to move.

'You're a brave man', I said as the doors closed; 'don't get stuck!'

I worked on the ninth floor a while moving a few things around and then took the stairs to eight. I set my things down on a ledge and recorded.

'Sweetie baby are you here? I thought I smelled your perfume a little bit.... On the eighth floor here'.... Oh excuse me. Do ghosts or demons fart... do you spirits go to the washroom, throw up, fight each other, get married have children or whatever?'

As I worked in the hallway by the back elevator room I flipped a door frame over, and doing that twisted a two by four piece of wood up against my left shin, just below the knee. I yelled out as I grabbed my leg and held my breath to help numb the initial pain.

'Damn that hurt…. You guys think that's funny?…… Not laughing at you guys not really', I said as I tried walking off the pain….. You don't think it's funny do you sweetie?…. Boo, boo'…

39} "THAT'S HOW YOU HURT YOURSELF"…

I finished up the eighth floor then took the grey striped stairwell down for lunch. During lunch Silvio informed me that the elevator was probably too dusty which is why it was working less and less. That didn't make sense to me but it didn't matter. I decided not to take it alone again. I walked up the grey striped stairwell to the seventh floor and kept recording as I worked my way down.

'Quarter after one and I'm on the seventh floor…. You guys don't mind me working back there do you? Back elevator room here. I gotta do it, sorry…… A couple of minutes and I'll be done'.

'Sixth floor, purple striped stairwell….. You guys alright? Anything I can do? Just let me know.'

I stopped recording to do some heavy dusty work, dragging material around to the elevators. I took the stairs to the main floor and left the motel in my air conditioned truck for a well deserved coffee.

One day at a time. One haunting at a time. I finished the week with a short e.v.p. session in the purple striped stairwell of the twenty fourth floor.

'Hey it's just me. Hope its okay to visit you guys. You guys cool? Everybody cool?…

40} "C'EST BON"……

'Alright.'…

"F*#K YOU, HEY F*#K YOU"…

'Ciao', I said as I stopped recording and took my time descending the grey striped stairwell, making sure I had the bag of small mementos to add to my collection from this sad oppressive place that the ghosts called their home in hell.

1} masculine-voice 2} feminine-whisper 3} masculine-whispers and voice 4} masculine-voice 5} masculine-whisper 6} masculine-voice 7} masculine-voice, whisper, voice 8} masculine-whispers 9} feminine-voice 10} masculine-voice, whisper, growl 11} masculine-voice 12} masculine-whisper 13} masculine-whisper 14} masculine-voice 15} feminine-whisper 16} masculine-voice 17} feminine-voice 18} masculine-voice 19} masculine-voice 20} masculine-voice 21} masculine-voice, snickering 22} masculine-voice 23} masculine-voice 24} masculine-voice 25} masculine-voices 26} masculine-voice 27} masculine-voice 28} feminine-whisper 29} masculine-voice 30} masculine-voice, feminine-voice, masculine-voice 31} masculine-voices 32} masculine-voice 33} masculine-voice 34} feminine-whisper 35} masculine-whispers 36} masculine-voice 37} masculine-voice 38} masculine-voice, masculine-whisper 39} masculine-voice 40} masculine-voices

↑   ↑

Peek -a- boo, I see you 'two'.

(In the black squares)

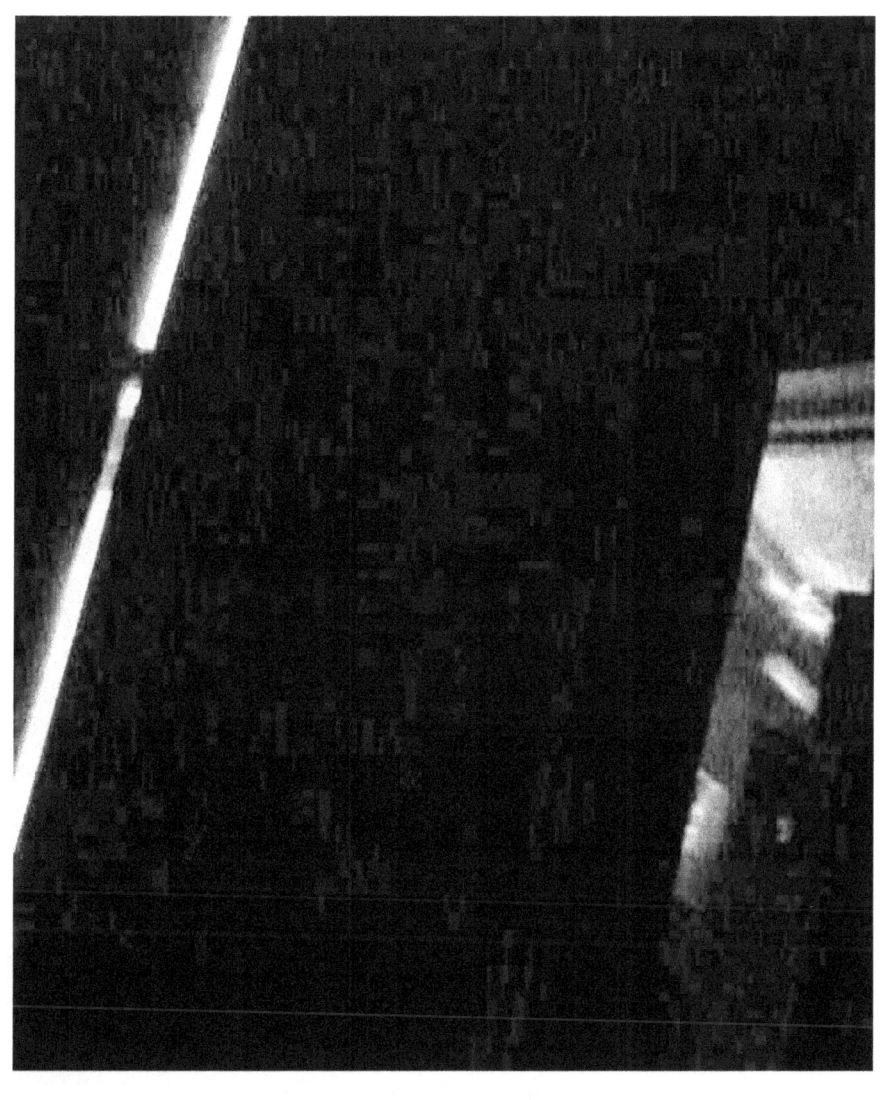

↑

Near the roof area of the motel. Looks like a gargoyle face.

Chapter Eight; It's You We Hate

Psalm 111: 10 **The fear of the LORD is the beginning of wisdom ….**

I arrived at work early Monday morning, giving myself time to relax and feel more awake while drinking my third cup of coffee. While I was sitting in my truck I noticed Matt pull into the parking spot across from my vehicle. He got out of his car and walked over to me saying;

'Morning buddy'. He held out his hand to shake mine.

'What's the handshake for', I asked, looking perplexed.

'I wanted to say that it was nice working with you but I'm just going to quit'.

'What how come, don't quit dude we need you here. Why quit at least wait for the lay offs you do know some of us will be laid off, probably this week'.

'Yeah I know, he said. I don't want to be here anymore, this place freaks me out Exi'. I'm going to save Silvio the trouble I know what I'm doing I'll be fine', he said as we shook hands.

'Are you sure man? I'll miss working with you but hey, God bless you man take care and stay out of trouble my friend'.

I watched him walk over to a few of the guys and Silvio standing by the back entrance to the motel. He said his goodbyes and left.

That was a bit of a surprise. I didn't think any of us would quit but thinking about it I realized the Skipper was one of the most frightened out of everybody here. I thought of when he was sent to the third floor to start collecting the smashed down block walls, but within the hour he was back on the fourth floor with the rest of us telling Silvio that he didn't want to work down there alone. He never spoke about it with me but something must have scared him. Last week Silvio had him working alone from the twentieth to the sixteenth floors and now all of a sudden he was quitting. It made me wonder how much spiritual attack he had really been exposed to from the ghosts.

I grabbed what I needed and made my way over to the back entrance walking through the doors and down the creepy hallway to my left, joining what was left of the crew in the back locker room. Today my work assignment was to organize the tools down in the old shower locker room where I had met Carey, the old maintenance man. Someone from the renovation company would be here in the next few days to collect a lot of the equipment and tools we no longer needed, so I did that in the morning then at lunch time joined Dario and Silvio down there for lunch for the last time. We were moving our tool room/lunch room back to the third floor now that the block walls were gone.

On Tuesday morning I was finishing up in the locker room area and this gave me a chance to video the old disco area. I began the video in a side room behind the bar, noticing a neon sign of a girl posing in a flirty manner. Next to her was a sign that used to be hanging in the main room, white writing on a black backdrop that read 'le Place'. I added them to my collection.

I walked out of that room back into the main room and viewed the different sections of the defunct night club with wires hanging from everywhere and the holes in some of the walls, the faint odour of chlorine and dampness all around. I could imagine back in time how much fun this place must have been, especially when the better bands and acts used to play. Even the bar was shaped like a parallelogram keeping with the shape of the exterior walls.

To my right was the entrance door to the bar leading in from the flight of stairs from the second floor. The stairwell was elegant in decor and had small mirrors on the ceiling creating a kind of reflective optical illusion as you walked down them.

After lunch I walked up the purple striped stairwell knowing the spirits were around. It was always a strange feeling. With all the hard work I was doing every day and all the heat and humidity, it was strenuous making that climb. I rested as I made my way up, stopping on the landings for water. Arriving on the floor I walked to the window and set the camera on a balcony window ledge facing the entrance to the purple striped stairwell and sat beside the camera for a quiet break as it recorded the thick aired silence.

When I finished the work I phoned Silvio for the elevator instead of wearing myself out, then while waiting I took a short video from the balcony, of the top of my truck and the sinister looking set of picnic tables formed into a circle across the street in the park.

I kept the video in the room across from the purple striped stairwell and then walked to it viewing the next landing. I walked down the hall a ways then turned and went back to the room.

1} "HOW COME YOU'RE SENDING US TO HELL?"...

I went to different windows to film yet another view.

2} "LET'S GO, NOT YET"...

There was a lot of greenery around the tower, surprising really considering all the different buildings built all around it.

3} "COME"………….. "COME TO ME,… PURE"…

I crouched in the room taping the room to my left then out to the right …

4} "LET HER GO"…

I wanted these images as a memory of this place. I got that for sure and than some. I finished my day filming a close up of the picnic tables in a circle in the park. I waited for Silvio to come get me and then went to the basement bar area where Dario helped me carry two green wicker tables out to my truck. I loaded them in the back and drove home with my new souvenirs. I put them in our storage space that evening.

I downloaded the most recent videos and reviewed them finding more faces and voices in the haunted motel.

Wednesday morning I was on the twenty sixth floor.

'Good morning', I said into the back room . 'Is there anybody here?'… 'Oh you might think that it's a bit goofy but the ghosts at the motel are spooky'. I wheeled the cart around, stacking the metal pipe pieces into it making up limericks as I worked.

'Where I work is a spooky place, I keep a smile on my face. I wear some crosses just in case, to keep the ghoulies in their place'…..

5} "YOU'RE NUT'S"…

'Might think that it's a bit goofy, but jackson I think that you're, kooky'…

6} "YEAH BABY"…

'Jackson, you're a freak, super freak, you're super freaking out… Waw ah, ah. She's a very spooky girl. The kind of ghost you don't take home to mother.'….

7} "I LOVE YOU".

I grabbed an end of a huge piece of duct work and tossed it down the opening in the floor where the stairs used to be. I watched it fall and land fifteen feet below. It made a loud bang …

8} "CAREFUL THERE".

Later I drove out for coffee and enjoyed the temporary reprieve of the air conditioning in the truck. After break I took my camera with me to the twenty fifth floor's back room to film the holes around the elevator while Silvio worked on the pipes from the scaffolding.

'Hey you savages are you in there'…

9} "WE'LL BE WATCHING"…

I was getting a lot of voices lately, almost daily actually. Around this time Rudy decided to quit. He and Silvio were butting heads as to his job assignments.

'Grandpa is getting on my nerves bro I'm leaving. Screw this haunted place anyways Exi, I'm outta here', he told me from his car that day after our last scheduled break.

He was the second person who hadn't waited for the layoff which was unfortunate but somewhat understandable. I believed the fact the motel was haunted had something to do with it. Working in the tower was oppressive to everyone in very different ways.

Thursday morning was the skeleton crew. Roy was outside and Silvio, Papa and I were in the tower. Papa was on the fourth floor hammering away at a wall. I had started forcing myself to take the middle elevator alone and got off on the fourth floor to ask Papa if he had seen Silvio.

'Hey Papa how are you have you seen Silvio?'

'No I haven't. What floor are you working on?'.

'I am on the twenty sixth floor by myself. It is spooky up there'.

He laughed.

'Come on up and check it out, we will have an easy day.'

I couldn't get a hold of Silvio. I think he was tired that day and wanted to hide. He deserved a rest. We all did.

Papa and me entered the elevator and went to floor twenty five in order to get to the stairs to get to twenty six. We got out on the twenty fifth and talked about the view though we couldn't see much due to the fog and the rain. We took the grey striped stairwell to the top floor and he looked around as we went to the small electrical room that led to the roof door.

Papa noticed a steel doored cubby hole and looked inside it and said; 'A hiding place'.

'That's where the ghost sleeps at night', I said as we laughed.

Papa never talked about the haunting so I never knew what he thought about it all.

'I am still looking for my shovel jackson, the big plastic one I haven't seen it for a while have you seen it anywhere?' I asked him.

'No I haven't'.

I pointed out the soot filled room as we took the stairs to twenty five. We took the elevator down to twenty one as I got out and asked Papa to wait for me while I looked for the shovel. I got out and walked around the floor as I quickly looked around. I looked in the back room as I walked by it….

10} "HEY, JUST LEAVE" …

'What the hell was that', I thought. I had actually just heard an audible voice. That totally stunned me. I quickened my pace and made it back to the elevator.

'Papa I swear I just heard a voice in the back room'.

'Yeah', he said chuckling. He must have thought I was crazy for sure.

'Just now man', I said as I flicked the service switch off.

'Yeah?' he said chuckling harder.

'I'm serious, I haven't heard one before that was the first time Papa and it freaks me out'

We rode back down to the fourth floor.

'If he bothers me up there I might have to knock him out'.

Papa just kept chuckling as we got to the floor wondering no doubt if I was serious or not. Couldn't blame him if he didn't believe me, I just hoped he had. I believe he did.

'See you man I am going to call Silvio.'

I went down to the main floor and Silvio got in. We rode up and I decided to tell him about the voice.

'I was looking for jackson on the twenty first floor, when I walked past the back elevators I heard a voice. Just now I'm serious.'

'A voice, he asked.

'A man's voice Silvio it creeped me right out.' He looked at me half asleep.

'Do you remember when Dario and me were loading some steel doors last week he was telling you about when that guy in the white hat came around the corner and scared him, he started telling us that the other guy the manager, that tall guy when he does his rounds he hears voices from in here.'

The elevator doors opened. 'So, just now I heard a voice. You know me by now buddy I am not crazy', I said.

Then Silvio said; 'Why maybe do you call to him to expose him too much?'

'That's okay I have the power', I said chuckling.

'Yeah, but you never know', he said. 'If I call Exi, Exi; eventually you are going to answer.'

'I don't know Silvio; I don't know what it is.'

11} "DIRTY ONE THING"...

'Come with me on the twenty first floor. Just once let's walk and see what happens' I said, 'and I can check the twenty second floor for jackson'.

We got out and walked around the floor listening intently as we passed the back room. Deep down I knew that he believed me. So much had affected Silvio in this place. He had shared his experiences with me so I knew.

'I don't care about working by myself I just don't want them scaring me like that', I said as we walked back to the elevators.

'I didn't hear anything', he said.

'Maybe on the next floor', I said as we got in the elevator and rode up to the twenty second floor.

'Jackson is the name of the guy to die in here?', he asked me.

'No I don't think so, that's just what I call him anyway, like the shovel'.

'Maybe jackson's spirit is here', he said.

We got out on the twenty second floor and walked around it then took the elevator to twenty five. We hadn't heard any audible voices. Silvio got out as I went to floors twenty thru seventeen in the hope of finding jackson. It would be quite difficult to work without that shovel.

I took the elevator down to floor twenty and started walking around it.

12} "I'M DONE".

'You ghoulies want to talk to me… Do you want to play is that what you were saying yesterday?. You are tough against the Lord eh we will see about that… He just might send you's to the pit of hell if you have to hurt me. No matter what you will be going down fast'.

I was totally creeped right out, now that I had actually heard a voice with my own ears, in real time. I knew this was all real a long time ago but now it hit my spirit head on. I wanted to know God's power and stay in control. I was being exposed to the ghosts trying to scare me on a daily basis. On the days I felt confident maybe the spirits were re - grouping to hone down on their strategy to scare me.

I didn't feel very confident today, just facing my fears of the unknown. I took the elevator to nineteen aware of the fact the ghosts could hear me.

'I'll have you sent to the pit of hell if you's bother me. I'm just having fun with you so just fair warnings don't mess with me.' I walked the floor, briskly; 'I will do what I have to do…. I will do it'

I entered the elevator and went down to eighteen…

13} "COME AND MEET MY FATHER"….

I walked the floor and got back in the elevator to the twenty fifth floor. Silvio was on the scaffold cutting and hammering off the pipes from the ceiling.

I gathered some plywood from around the floor and got it organized. The elevator button buzzed and Dace got out. Thank goodness. I didn't feel like working alone today. We waved at each other from across the long floor. He looked tired; he must have been hanging drywall last night. As I walked past the stairwells I sang; 'good bye ghoulies. Good bye ghoulies'….

14} "YOU'RE TOUGH".

I walked up the grey striped stairwell to twenty six.

'Hey guys sorry about this morning.... Forgive me?... You know they took jackson on me eh.... jackson is gone, to a different job site.... jackson's a good guy'....

I had a smoke break on the roof. I opened the door and sat on the door step. Some drops of water dripped from the door frame and splashed my face.

'What's that? You guys crying on me or what that was weird'...

15} "NOT CRYING"...

I ate part of my lunch in the truck and finished the rest of it on the twenty fifth floor looking out into the dissipating fog thinking of my bizarre morning experience. I turned and spoke to them.

'Hey guys, I'm leaving. We've been instructed me and my brother Dace to clean the main floor in the back hallway on the way to the long exit there near the old chute, the ground floor. So if you's want to meet us there fine, okay? We're having fun today ooh, hee haw'.

The elevator doors opened and I leaned over to grab my things.

'We are leaving now we're getting off this floor, no more twenty three'...

16} "HA, HA, HA, HA, HA"...

I entered and pushed the button. As the doors closed I said; 'Later'. It was good to be getting off the higher floors to work in the cooler rooms.

17} "HECK NO".

'Any body in the elevator here with me'?... 'sweetie are you here? Who are you anyway somebody's wife? I have a feeling, some guy doesn't like me because of you and me. My wife's jealous of you too....

I stepped out of the elevator to the main floor. Dace had already brought some polished pieces of wood out from the room. He was keeping them for one of his projects. I walked to my left and noticed a flat dolly had been loaded with odds and ends so I wheeled it down to the door frame. It wouldn't fit through so I had to transfer it to another cart on the other side.

18} "WATCH OUT FOR ME"…

Silvio, Dace and I worked down there most of the afternoon, going through a lot of stuff stored and held onto over the years at the Park Sets Motel. We rummaged through a box filled with various items.

I also went through the boxes of artifacts near the side entrance.

19} "YOU'RE NO BAD MAN".

I separated what was trash and put the rest aside so we could go through it before the end of the day.

20} "STOP"…

Dace came down the hall with more junk.

'Alright lots of stuff'.

'Yeah dude', he said.

After emptying dollies and carts for an hour I was caught up with the work so made my way into the crowded back room where Dace was helping Silvio organize, mostly what was wood from trim to doors, shelved about ten square feet in a corner of the room. I squeezed my way in and Dace and I took turns sliding the pieces out for sorting. A lot of the wood was expensive but they were odds and ends so were all being thrown out.

21} "WHAT DO YOU WANT"… (SPIT) … "THE DEVIL, URGH".

Dace handed the pieces to me and I left them for Silvio to look over. I found what looked like an old silk bed sheet and I handed it to Silvio.

'Ah see, take it home and wash it, put it on your bed and dream of ghosts. Succubus will come and get you though'.

He thought about what I had just said; 'I'm gonna sleep like that and say come on'.

I laughed at his humour then said; 'As long as she is not an old hag right?'

22} "HERE BOSS"……"WHERE'S IT KEPT?" … "WHAT THE F*#K" …… "URGH", …. "YEAH"…

It was much cooler down in the basement in the late afternoon. We were finding different artifacts like old tools, plumb lines and chains and old ball peen hammers. We even found some brand new white visor head caps with 'Park Sets Motel' written on the front, but mostly it was just a whole lot of wood the place had hoarded over the years. As I went back to work alone in the corner, I sang a song that I guessed was not the ghosts favorite;

'Oh happy day, oh happy day. Oh happy day, oh happy day, when Jesus washed my sins away.'

23} "CUT IT OUT"…

Silvio was looking through a row of laminate sheets.

'I had a friend back home who died working with this stuff. He was working in a factory and was untying a bundle and a piece dislodged and cut his throat. He just bled to death.'

'Wow Silvio that's terrible, sorry man', I said.

We worked in silence for a while, deep in thought after that story.

Dace and I eventually wheeled the full dollies out to the side entrance then went back and did what we could in the storage room to pile the remaining scrap wood onto another dolly. Silvio had left so I made my way around the back hallway near the room, looking for him …. 'Silvio'?

I walked off down the long hallway leading to the old locker rooms to check if he was there.

24} "COME BACK"…

I wanted to let him know I was taking home some strips of gold painted wooden trim that I had found in todays clean up. I walked out to the side entrance and took the afternoon break in the shade feeling grateful for the great weather and more souvenirs for my collection. One hour to go. It had been an exhausting day and spiritually draining.

I wanted to review the voice I had heard this morning and any other voices I might have recorded. I wanted to see Tina and tell her about my haunted day and just how much she meant to me. I also wanted more peace of mind and confidence at work, more control on how I let the ghosts scare me. Maybe they weren't so mean after all. I would soon find out that I would be surrounded by more evil than I could have imagined.

1} masculine-voice 2} masculine, feminine-whispers 3} feminine-voice 4} masculine-voice 5} masculine-voice 6} masculine-voice 7} feminine-voice 8} masculine-voice 9} masculine-voice 10} masculine-voice 11} masculine-voice 12} masculine-voice 13} feminine-whisper 14} masculine-voice 15} masculine-voice 16} masculine chuckles 17} masculine-voice 18} masculine-whisper 19} masculine-voice 20} masculine-voice 21} masculine-voice, spit, masculine-voice 22} masculine-voice, growl 23} masculine-voice 24} masculine-voice

↑　↑
The stairs leading down to the old night club. Pretty wild looking customer(s).

The masked bandit again and his friends.

(In the black squares)

Chapter Nine; Running Out Of Time

1st Timothy 4: 1 **Now the Spirit speaketh expressly, that in the latter times some shall depart from the faith, giving heed to seducing spirits, and doctrines of devils.**

Why would spirits say things like that? Had we done anything to deserve their evil? Were they really threatening or were they saying things because they knew I was recording their voices, that it might scare me?

It did scare me and made me feel all the more oppressed. They were unusual things to say for sure. Like most of the audio I had recorded they were clear and understandable class A e.v.p.'s. At least some of the ghosts were diabolically evil hearted if they even had hearts. I remember feeling defeated. At this point in the haunting I believed the demons at the Park Sets Motel hated me and wanted me dead. Something had tried to hurt me on more than one occasion and couldn't care less whether I lived or died.

I struggled with my conscience that night debating whether or not I should tell Silvio about the audible noises I had been recording.

'That is plain evil, crazy, weird', I said to Tina after she had heard the recorded voices.

'Wow, that's unreal', she said. 'If I hadn't heard it with my own ears I might not believe it. I think they know what scares you Exi. From my own experiences I know they lie when they feel like it and ghosts enjoy confusing people and scaring people as much as they can. They can't seem to help themselves'.

'I think you are right. I feel bad but I don't think it would be a good idea telling Silvio or Dace about this. It's just too crazy and you know how superstitious Silvio is. Probably better for everyone if I don't say anything.'

'You know you could just do a kind of cleansing of the building. I have some holy water brought back from Jordan that you can use as part of a ritual to rid the place of evil spirits'.

'I don't know Tina. The thought of doing an exorcism on the tower scares the hell out of me, it truly freaks me out. I wouldn't want to do it alone either. That is never a good idea from what I've heard. You know I've already asked a few of the guys to help me deal with them but everyone's frightened of whatever's in there, so I'm on my own. Even though I know God has protected me so far it's hard to get my head around all of this. I'm not sure if he even wants me to do it. I'm gonna have to pray about it and wait and see. They could be trying to suck me into their drama and hurt me again. Sometimes when in doubt do nothing.'

'I know you are worried' she replied. I have an idea. If you want I can record a prayer on the device, that way if you ever feel led to get rid of them you won't be alone. They will hear you and me as well.'

'Thanks sweetheart, I appreciate your help. I will let you know about that. I have a lot of thinking to do'.

That night I struggled trying to sleep with the knowledge that the spirits from the other side might want to hurt someone again. I didn't feel scared anymore. I felt angry and stressed. Maybe that was a good thing though. Hopefully I would know what to do in the morning. Either tell at least Silvio about the recorded voices or I don't know, not say anything I guessed. One thing I did know was the diabolical were waiting for me everyday to come and visit them. I felt like quitting but that would mean the bullies at the motel had won and had chased me out and had scared off another human.

I did feel like quitting but as I finally fell asleep I decided it would be on my terms, not because some invisible nut bags were freaking out around me like a bunch of lunatics. I would try to stay in control.

I didn't exactly wake up feeling refreshed and confident the next morning. I was dragging myself around the apartment struggling to wake up, knowing I had to do or say something to deal with the spiritual attack at the motel.

Driving to work I told myself that every spirit feels fear even the scary ones. I tried to convince myself that the ghosts were afraid too, maybe more than me. I'll just be more assertive and stand my ground. We had a right to be there too.

I parked the truck and made my way through the main back hall towards the front foyer where I noticed Silvio tying his work boot. I thought of the only thing to say.

'Good morning boss. How are you Silvio? I don't think it is a good idea for any one of us to work alone anymore.'

'You don't want to work alone?'

'No I don't mind really that's not a problem. I just think we should start working in pairs just in case anything happens. It would just be safer that's all.'

'Something happen to scare you or something? You are acting strange'.

'No man I am just trying to be safe that's all.'

'Are you sure?'

'Yeah I am okay, you okay?

'Yeah I am good', he said chuckling.

'If anything weird happens you feel free to come and ask for my help my friend, okay?'

'Yeah sure man. You are one crazy guy', he said laughing. Just go up on fifteen. You know what to do. Just remember if you use the elevator don't press number nine or you will get stuck'.

'Thanks for telling me. Wow man can't they fix the elevators? This place is too much. I am going to take the stairs. I'm not taking any chances right now'.

'No problem', he said as he pressed the elevator button.

'K dude, see you up there,' I said as I watched the doors close. ' Time for some exercise'.

I walked to the grey striped stairwell already feeling oppressed hopeful that things would turn out for the best.

At least I had said something. I tried with the safety issue and that's all I could do for now under the circumstances. I started my climb up the dungy purple striped stairwell.

'Hey Dace', I called out as I reached the eighth floor. No answer. I wanted to say good morning to one of my haunted brothers but he hadn't shown up yet.

I climbed to the twelfth floor where I knew Dario had been working his way down using a small jack hammer in the back shaft room in an effort to remove the thin floor tiles glued to the floor.

'Yeah, it even smells like death', I mumbled as I reached the floor.

I walked around to the back and saw Dario.

'Dario what's up?'

'Not much just cutting these pieces down and I'm gonna chip the tiles, how about you?'.

'Well there's only one elevator working and since I've been stuck already I'm just taking my time and gonna take the stairs to the fifteenth and I'm going to be up there for a while. Did Silvio tell you about the elevator? If you press nine you get stuck and you can't put it on service.'

'All right buddy thanks have a good one', he said as I walked to the grey striped stairwell and continued my climb. I got to the floor and made my way to the back of the tower where I had left a broom for a final clean up of the floor.

1} "STEADY"…

While sweeping I asked; 'If any of you are here, what are your names?'…

2} "SMELL IT"….

As I worked I talked to the ghosts knowing they were near. Ghosts are not omnipresent; they can only be in one place at one time.

'Yeah you guys will just have to adapt to your new surroundings. Cause we are just the workers, that's all we are.'

They were creeping me out, my fear getting the better of me. ...

3} "WELL, WELL, WELL, WELL, WELL"...

The work load was easier now. The floors were now wide open allowing the daylight to brighten up the floors, more now than in the beginning. It allowed the healing rays of the sun to touch the core of the tower and provided more room to run from anything that might want to harass me.

I was constantly recording and keeping up with reviewing the evidence I was finding. It was important for me to know as much as possible as to what they might be up to. I made sure to start recording first thing in the mornings to keep up with the increasing activity in the tower.

I spent the day up on floor fifteen, not over exerting myself on another sizzling hot day. Driving home that afternoon I was still on edge but relieved to have left the haunted work site.

The next day I climbed up the grey striped stairwell to the third floor where we all gathered in the mornings.

4} "WHAT'S UNDER THAT"....

Silvio had us scattered about the tower. I got out with Dace on the tenth floor where he had been working. We talked a few minutes and then, I started feeling sick.

'Oh man I don't feel so well, am I ever dizzy', I said as I crouched up against a wall.

'You gonna be alright dude?'.

'Wow I don't know I hope so', I said, staying still, waiting for the room to stop moving.

5} "YOU'RE GONNA... DIE".

When my dizziness finally subsided, I took the purple striped stairwell stairs to the fifteenth floor to continue a final clean up of the floor.

I greeted the ghosts as I reached the floor; 'Good morning you goof balls'.

'What do you think of this one; 'Love is God, sent his son. Love forgives all we have done'. In this world, where hatred seems to grow true love goes against the flow, and becomes so hard to show. Lord we need to know the power of your love'.

6} "LET IT GO"….

'Are any of you abnormal, I always wondered about that if you demons are deformed in any way…. This next song is for sweetie; 'do, do, do, do, I had a ghost and sweetie was her name, bo, bo, bo, bo, now that she's gone, I never felt the same, cause I love my sweetie do, do, do, do, do. 'She should have been with God, she chose this life alone, and now you walk around, you haunt those in your home.'

I took a break before singing an Alice Cooper classic.

'Plastic forks and spoons, no laces in my shoes, they all know what I tried to do, outside the quiet room'. ('Wa, wa, wa, wa, wa') 'how long have I been gone' ('how long have I') 'did winter kill the lawn' ('winter kill the lawn') 'and all those polaroids you sent, are on the wall in the quiet room'. 'They've got this place, where they've been creeping me'….

7} "PERFECT… NOW"…..

… 'where I can't hurt myself, I can't get my wrists to bleed, just don't know why, suicide, appeals to me'. 'The quiet room, is sterilized and white, it's like a tomb, with just a moth stained naked night.'

'Did you like it? Whew! Alice Cooper, Alice Cooper is a trooper. Son of a Baptist preacher, praise the Lord …… and repentance brings a man to salvation amen? Well, except for you ghoulies. You know that you will be in the lake of fire, whew! Then you will know you are hot you harassers. I will harass you too, in the name of the Lord.'….

8} "OH YEAH"...

I took another break then I played a game to get them going.

'We are going to play word of the day; word of the day is what shall it be? Word of the day... Shall be... Transition!... Transition! Transition for all you demons; from walls and memories, to no walls and memories.... 'I really appreciate the warning you gave me oh yeah. Thank you. Thank you very much...

9} "UH HUH"...

'Sweetie are you here?'...

I was angry at them. It had been building up and I didn't care that I was taunting them.

I noticed it was almost break time. I finished cleaning the back shaft room. I had to use a washroom and no way would I make it down all the stairs in time, so I picked a pile of dust like a cat in a large litter box.

'I am going to mark my territory.... So you can smell it'....

I took the grey striped stairs down for the morning break feeling like I had won the first round of the day.

I drove for a coffee and enjoyed the small reward. Before heading back up I grabbed my lunch bag. I decided to have my lunch up in the tower instead of wearing myself out, constantly taking the stairs.

I continued sweeping the hall relieved I had shut the door to the purple striped stairwell.

'I'm trying to stay out of your stairwell'.

I had the very familiar feeling that something was around me.

'I have a feeling somebody's here. Some of you here with me right now?... answer me fourteenth floor hooligans'...

'Honey are you there? sweetie? sweetie pie?... Which one of you is named jackson. What are some of your names? ..... Don't be shy. I want to hear from you. Everyone should be heard.'

'Why do you hate me? Is it because I taunt you? Is it me or the cross?'.........

I finished cleaning around the back room as quickly as I could. It's where the ghosts literally seemed to be 'hanging out'. I took a quick break to rest. I decided to mark my territory again and used another pile of dust.

'Gonna pee now mark my territory..... You guys like holy water? Straight from the Jordan.... I have some if you guys are thirsty. It's hot baby whew.'

'Sweetie are you here?.... Fourteenth floor.... What do you hooligan's do with your time anyway?......

10} "DO WHAT?".....

'Hang out with everybody?'......

11} "LET ME KNOW"....

12} "I THOUGHT YOU LOOKED CUTE"....

'So where are all of you from? Were you born here or did you die here?..... I know you can talk... And like scaring the heck out of people but besides that I don't know what's up'....

13} "EDGE OF THE PIT NOW"....

14} "BEAUTIFUL BOY".... "URRGH"

'Here they come here they come the ghosts are lots of fun.'... 'You guys like that one, it's pretty funny'...

15} "GONNA WATCH YOU"...

I took my time working in the early afternoon heat.

As I gave a final sweep of the back room I asked; 'Do you guys feel heat or cold?.... Do you all live up there', I said looking at the partially opened and exposed back elevator door...

16} "YOU WIN".....

'Do you like it better dirty or clean? It's pretty hot out there so I guess your in hell so there you go it makes sense'…..

I went down to my truck grateful for the air conditioning. As I slowly cooled off I had some juice and ate my lunch. I noticed Tina had sent me a text message.

'Well I just survived an earthquake wow it felt weird. I love you'.

An earthquake? I hadn't felt a thing and I had been on the fourteenth floor. I called her at work and turned the radio on for the news.

'Hey there bella. So what's this about an earthquake?' I asked her.

She explained that she was at her desk and the two story building she worked in started shaking. I told her that I was on the fourteenth floor but hadn't felt anything. Knowing she was alright I finished my lunch, then went and asked a few of the guys sitting outside the entrance if they had noticed the earthquake. Roy said he felt some shaking but the rest of us in the tower hadn't noticed.

I made my way back up. As I was getting ready to start working I noticed two men with white hats on walking around the corner towards where I was standing. One of them was an engineer. He said hello then asked if I had felt the earthquake.

'No I said. I just spoke with my wife and she told me about it'.

'See how strong the old tower is. She is old but tough and strong' he said.

I finished the last hour of the work day grateful once again for quitting time.

It was hard getting back into the swing of things after four days off, and I made sure to rest up that weekend and relaxed as much as I could.

I took it easy in the sweltering temperatures inside the tower the following week. It was like a sauna in there, quite unbearable really.

I got in the elevator with Dace.

'Don't press nine or eight', I said.

'No, I don't mess with those two numbers bro'.

'What floor are you on brother'? I asked.

'I'm on seven'.

'I'm on ten. I am catching up to you'.

We stepped out on the seventh floor where Papa was getting ready to start his day. They were both hammering the loose Styrofoam™ off of the concrete walls. It was brutal work really and I was glad I hadn't been assigned to do it.

'I am taking the stairs from here', I told Dace. He laughed knowing I didn't take the elevators alone if I could help it.

I walked up to the tenth floor.

'Good morning you hooligan's…. I do not feel like talking to you today… But I'm going to anyway…I'm getting used to talking to you anyway'.

'What's in a name that makes the demons flee, in the name of Jesus name above all names'……

'You demons know that right, amen?'

I could feel them more on some days than others and this was one of those days.

I sang some contemporary music I had learned. As the days went by at the tower I noticed how much more at peace I felt as I sang, almost as if it was keeping the evil at bay. Maybe they felt groggy almost comatose while I did.

Another fact about these ghosts I was learning was that they were everywhere.

Later in the day I asked Silvio when they were going to lay me off.

'That's what I wanted to talk to you about. Hector told me that you and Papa and Roy this week will be the last week.'

'I was the first one here I should be the last one to go. I need the money too.'

'I don't know Exi' he said.

'Do you mind if I stay?' I asked him.

'No. I told Hector you were a good worker, it doesn't matter to me that way.'

He gave me his number and I programmed it into my phone. I waited about ten minutes and then called Hector, hoping to be able to straighten it out. I didn't want to be laid off at least not yet.

Dario and I had no children. Dace had four kids. Keeping Dace would be the right thing to do for that reason alone, besides that I was staying if I could help it.

I got his voice mail and left him a brief message.

Well, that was that I guessed. I walked up to Dace's floor and we discussed the layoff. It was frustrating thinking I was getting taken advantage of and losing my needed income though I was glad they were keeping Dace and Dario.

I went to my truck to restock on water and granola bars and then climbed the stairs again, disappointed that I might be leaving the haunted tower sooner than I had wanted.

I worked my way down the floors from the tenth to the sixth. It was time consuming but easy work.

'Well I guess I am laid off. I guess you guys are happy about that; all you demons,' I said to my invisible foes.

I knew I would miss them. They had given me one of the most memorable times of my life all be it insane and surreal. I wished I had gotten more video of the grand haunted building. The voices, whispers and grunts I have recorded are truly creepy and I believe the pictures speak for themselves.

I also have a scar on my wrist as a reminder of my time at the Park Sets Motel. I went down to the next floor and reflected on the last few months in silence....

17} "WHY DON'T YOU BRING IT TO THE BIG BOSSES"....

It was almost two o'clock, quitting time. I gathered my things and walked down the stairs to the hallway leading out to the back doors. Dario was in his van and motioned me to come over.

'Have you seen Silvio, I think he was looking for you. Something about you working on Monday'.

'Oh yeah? That's good. I was coming back just in case but that's great and thanks for telling me Dario. Have a good weekend, see you on Monday'.

As I started the truck Silvio called and told me to come back on Monday. I was grateful for the reprieve. I would have missed the guys and the work. But I would have missed the ghosts the most.

The powers that be made it so I would stay and continue to fight the good fight. It was a spiritual challenge to me to try and solve some of the mysteries surrounding all these spirits and I was given the chance to keep recording the ghosts amidst all the changes in their lives. The twilight zone called the Park Sets Motel would engulf me for a little while longer.

1} masculine-voice 2} masculine-voice 3} masculine-whisper 4} masculine-voice 5} masculine-voices 6} masculine-voice 7} masculine-voice 8} masculine-voice 9} masculine-voice 10} feminine-whisper 11} masculine-whisper 12} feminine-whisper 13} masculine-voice 14} feminine-whisper, growl 15} masculine-voice 16} masculine-voice 17} masculine-voice.

↑   ↑   ↑

Some beast faces hanging 'in' the purple striped stairwell.

Chapter Ten; Hi, I Want A Friend

John 3: 16 *For God so loved the world, that he gave his only begotten Son, that whosoever believeth in him should not perish, but have everlasting life.*

Another glorious long weekend was here. I slept in on Friday until noon and it felt great to rest. A person really needs a good sleep at least once a month I think; at least I do if I can find the time. Tina was at work so I moseyed about the apartment enjoying the air conditioning. I eventually got around to painting the den. I applied the first coat to the walls, a relaxing green color called Shenandoah Valley.

That evening Tina and I watched a movie. She went to bed early so I stayed up and watched a baseball game. On Saturday morning we drove an hour west to visit one of my sisters, Glenda at her trailer park to enjoy the day relaxing in the sun and did some swimming in the small man made pond. My Aunt Nell also had a trailer there and we had planned to surprise my mother for her eightieth birthday with a party on Sunday. It was a milestone for her. My mother had made it to eighty. She is the oldest of her large family. Her four sisters were there on her special day along with some of her children, some nephews and nieces, and grand children.

I was feeling relieved that I was still needed at the motel and as I drove to work on Monday I wondered how much longer they would keep me. I figured I had about a month. I parked the truck in its familiar spot. I got there early and relaxed waiting for Silvio to arrive. When he arrived I walked over to the cars.

'Morning dog', I said to Dace.

'Morning' he replied sleepily. Dog was the nickname we had respectfully given him on account of the way he worked, tough and hard like a dog would.

I walked to the back doors where Dace and Dario were talking while waiting for Silvio to unlock the wooden door.

'Hey Exi what's happening?' Dario said.

'Good morning Dario'.

'What's up brother Exi ready to rumble?' Dace said.

'Oh yeah always bro'. I was glad to be back.

1} "STILL SOMEBODY HERE"...

We waited a few more minutes then Silvio walked over and let us in. We made our way to the elevator and rode our way up to the third floor where we slowly but surely all did what we had to do to start the day. Silvio voiced what he wanted us to do. Dario and Dace were on the twenty first floor working on cutting the huge drainage pipes which were hanging beside the wall in the back elevator shaft room.

They were working right beside a hole cut out in the elevator shaft cinder block wall where I had videoed pictures of the ghosts. I hadn't told anyone that I knew the ghosts were in there.

I started my day on the nineteenth floor and started recording while narrating;

'Thursday July fifteenth my wife's birthday. So what do you ghoulies have to say for yourselves…? Morning. How are you guys?…. We're almost done. Are you happy?…. It's all coming together. Are you guys ready for the pit?'........

I sang a short song;

'Today's your birthday gonna have a good time'. I took the stairs down.

'Nineteenth floor to the eighteenth floor…. Oh yeah it's going to be a hot one…. You guys affected by heat and humidity?..… Probably don't like it much it probably reminds you of hell…. I'm sure you've heard a lot about it haven't you'….

I walked to the stairs;

'Alright purple striped stairwell going down to seventeen…. Footprints in the concrete'. I walked around the floor; 'Sweetie are you here today?

2} …. "HI"….

'Talk to me baby'….

"I'D LIKE TO"….

'What's going on?.... What's happening?.. Ciao for now'.

I continued recording later in the morning. I checked a text message Tina had just sent me.

'Yee haw just got a message from my sweetheart'…..

3} "MY BIRTHDAY TOO"…..

It was extremely hot in the tower even with all the windows opened.

'What do you ghoulies have to say for yourselves? Are you going to miss us? …. You know I had to use some of these floors as a washroom right?…. Maybe I'll get lucky and I won't have to clean it I don't know, don't tell anybody okay?'…….

4} "OKAY"…

'You demon ghoulies. You guys should tell me some of your names you know my name… My wife's name is Tina, I'm Exi. It's her birthday today she is thirty six. What are your names….. How old are some of you'? ….

I went down to my truck and grabbed my lunch then went back up to eat it in the tower.

'Twelfth floor July fifteenth'…..

5} "I'M SMELLING IT"…

'Casper the friendly ghost the friendliest ghost we know'…

6} "HELP ME"…

The afternoon sailed along quickly as another work day ended.

Friday was a shorter day at work as we were now leaving at two p.m. Before I left that day I had a message for the demons on the floor.

'I just drew crosses by all the exits, stairways, elevators and back room. What do you guys think of that? ... See you guys on Monday. You ghoulies have a good weekend, ciao'.

It might seem nasty to some of you readers how I talked to the ghosts but I wasn't trying to be. I was intimidated by them, frightened of the unknown like I think most people would be. That treatment was my way of not allowing them the control. I tried to put on God's armour everyday but that was always difficult, me being imperfect and all. But I said and did what I thought I had to. I was doing my best to get through the haunting in the Park Sets Motel.

That Saturday morning as Tina and I had our coffees we discussed what we wanted to do for the day. She mentioned that we could go visit the tower as she hadn't seen it in person. We brought a lunch and sat in the park across from the motel, did some e.v.p. work, took some video of the concrete giant and some of the park.

We were looking forward to our afternoon and I was looking forward to showing her the building from a distance at least. We drove there in the mid afternoon first stopping for soup and coffee, then parked the truck and walked a short distance to the group of picnic tables in the shape of a circle to eat our lunch and try to make contact with the spirit world. Tina started the session.

'July seventeenth at the park across from the Park Sets Motel' ...

7} "COME FOR ME"...

'Is there any body here... Do you guys ever come outside of the building........ Has anybody died in this park......... Has anything bad happened in this park............. Do you guys like my husband Exi?........ I want to wish you a belated happy birthday'.....

'How many of you guys are here… If you are here please give us a sign, make some noise. (The wind started blowing as Tina said that.) We just want to talk to you…. We want to help you just let us know what happened, why are you here'? …

8} "WHERE ARE YOU MOMMY?"…… "MOMMY"

'I'm going to tape this for just another minute……. Goodbye'.

Tina took a brief video of the tall motel looking into the open windows of the twelfth floor where I had been on Friday.

'I'll do a little bit of a video and see if any of our ghoulie friends are up there waving at us. Here I'll wave at them, hi; I can see the double window that's open up there'.

We went for a walk and climbed a high narrow set of stairs that led up to the busy intersection and then circled our way back down into the park to where the truck was parked.

We had a barbecued meal and sat on our balcony that night, sipping on Tina's father's home made red wine and taking in the brightly lit up lights of the city sky line off in the distance.

Monday morning arrived too soon. I drove to work with all the other commuters in heavy traffic, driving the familiar route to work with a forecasted hot humid day ahead.

I started more audio recordings after my lunch, leaving the recorder run as I started working on the eighth floor …..

9} "I'M VINCENT"…..

I later took the stairs down to the seventh floor and chatted with Dace a few minutes and asked him if the ghosts were leaving him alone.

'I just try to ignore them bra. I listen to my music and chill out' he said.

'Good stuff I hear you brother' I replied.

I walked back up to the eighth floor glad in knowing Dace was hanging in there. At about three o'clock I called Tina at work from my cell phone on the eighth floor.

'Calling my sweetheart at work, my wife Tina.'……

The phone rang as I waited.

'Hello there, just taking a break and calling you. How is your day going?…. I try to be careful no worries'.

Tina then told me that someone she knew had written a book about ghosts.

'Oh he wrote one?…….. Well, that should be interesting.….. Right on that should be good.….. I went over to the park at lunch time and did a little session,… Yeah a couple of minutes just like you did on Saturday. I asked them if any of you guys remember where I went to the washroom in this place because I can't find the piles, just to get them going…. I'll see if they answer, I don't know…….. Well I'm just about ready for anything working here so don't worry, they're the ones that need to start worrying………. Did you have a good sleep?... Right on……… Oh your enjoying that, a nice change for you huh?.... That's a good thing I'm glad for you………

'Yes I asked Silvio this morning so I guess we'll pretty much be done the end of the week cleaning up and what not'. He said no, we have to do in front of the elevators. It's not a very big section but all the way down, knock down the plaster and there's probably metal up there that kind of thing you know, like holding it up.….. Probably another week at least so that's good… Oh, okay bye for now.'

10} "IT'S NOT THIS ONE"…

'My wife is sweet but she's a demon warrior … What do you guys think of that?'……

Then I sang an improvised song.

'Casper the demon ghost, friendliest demon we know'…… 'Do do do do do'.

'One elevator working… Out of three, out of two actually. Not good'.

I stared out into the massive park land.

'It's like central park over there, wow…….. Who was asking for help on Saturday?.....

11} "NOT I"…

"LOOK AT HIM, LOOK"….

'Any body here?.... Everybody alright?'....

I wrapped up my days work and made the walk down the stairs and drove home.

That night I went through the audio again that Tina and I had recorded at the park. We were blown away at the voice that said 'come for me'. It was the voice of a little girl clear as could be and it sounded echoed like it was in the air or the trees. I reviewed the audio I had taken that day. I was always amazed at what they were saying but not shocked. I was used to getting something almost daily, but they are always whacky things to hear.

The next morning I arrived at work and walked the familiar path into the side entrance then the winding hallway to the passenger elevators.

'Good morning Dario'.

'Hey Exi how are you bud?'

'Tired man really, how you doing?'

'I'm feeling worn out too. We're still cutting those pipes then bringing them downstairs. It's not that difficult but kind of dirty though'.

We waited by the elevators then Dace came down the hallway.

'Good morning alleluia, the Lord you know!'

We stepped into the elevator.

'What floor we on Dario, nine?'

'Yeah nine', Dario replied.

'I'm counting down the days I'm hoping for this week at least' Dace said.

We arrived on the eighth floor.

'Yes brother Exi', Dace said.

'Back to the ghoulies', I replied.

At break time I stayed up in the tower and called Tina.

I shut my phone off then accidentally dropped it.

'I dropped my phone', I said as I picked it up to check if it was damaged aware that the ghosts at the Park Sets Motel were listening. It was okay.

'Excuse me ghoulies'……..

12} "I TRUST HIM"………

"NO"….

'Ghoulies I know you are here'.

They were creeping me out yet again.

I was getting used to knowing when a spirit was near me.

'Alright eighth floor swept and finished' I said as I smacked my gloves against a wall. 'Well there's a fly buzzing around that's a good sign, a sign of life even though they were once maggots.'

Whatever I could think of to say or do I just threw it out there into their lazy world.

I worked as fast as I could. I could literally feel something around me and couldn't wait to get off the oppressive twelfth floor. It had given off a negative spiritual vibe for a long time.

'I'm going to the sixth floor after this in case you's are interested'.

'This is the twelfth, I'm going on the eighth and then I'm going to the sixth and ah, you can find me I'm sure. Just look for the medium sized cross on my back, the cross of Calvary the small one on my chest, and a large one in my heart amen?

'Thank you Jesus'.

As I swept I thought of how little time was left for me in the huge motel.

I wheeled the barrow to the elevator then walked to the back shaft and smacked the dust off of my gloves against a wall and said;

'As they would say in a poltergeist movie, this house is clean dudes.'…..

13} "AT CHURCH"……

14} "GET OUT"…

I walked around the floor checking that it was completely cleaned then sat on a window ledge and had a short break.

15} "OH YEAH I'M NOT SUPPOSE TO WATCH YOU"

After lunch I worked on the sixth floor as I continued recording.

16} "HIM"….

It's interesting how some of the voices and sentences made sense though many did not. The day Roy left he mentioned how evil the purple striped stairwell seemed to him. He heard voices while walking passed it even though no one was there.

17} "I WARNED YOU"…

The pipes made a loud noise as I dragged them, somehow making me feel more powerful. I was physically strong and ready for any of the ghost's tactics or at least I tried to convince myself of that.

Suddenly I noticed a shadow out of the corner of my eye. The whole morning was feeling uncomfortable and now the afternoon was as well.

'You ghoulies on the sixth floor just now did you guy's try and ah, freak me out? Why would you do that? Like a shadow right in front of the elevator. If you're trying to scare me I'll give you some advice; don't. Cause I can scare you real bad. If you're just passing through, fine'.

During my afternoon break I went to the back elevator shaft on the second floor and filmed the two storey foyer then went to my truck for water then once again climbed the purple striped stairwell to the fourth floor.

18} "STOP IT".

The next morning I made my way to the grey striped stairwell.

I exited to the seventh floor to continue working. First I opened all the windows. I started collecting the smaller pipes.

'Bringing the pipes over'….

19} "CAN'T PUT THEM THERE"…

    "OF COURSE YOU CAN"…

    "I DON'T KNOW"…

I found an old magazine in a pile of debris which I ended up keeping.

It took me half an hour to finish then I checked six and realized it was done. Dario showed up and we had a short conversation.

'Hey bud', I said.

'What's happening Exi'.

'I was just thinking, while I was dragging one of those pipes this morning it snapped in half. If I hadn't moved my stomach, it would have cut me open like gutting a fish. Pretty scary actually, it's not hard getting hurt in this place'.

He told me a story about when he was a kid, a friend of his was playing baseball and got hit in the head by a bat. It cracked his skull open. They had to press on his head while taking him to the hospital because his brain was leaking out. He turned out to be okay surprisingly enough. The same guy years later was in an auto accident and flew through the windshield. He had a lot of glass imbedded into his head. A few months later and the glass was still working its way out of his skull. He survived the accident but is still picking slivers of glass from his head. Strange but true.

We finished our conversation and I took the stairs to five and began carrying and dragging the remaining cut pipes to the elevator entrance.

On Thursday I started recording after my first scheduled break. I climbed the stairs to the third floor where I had been working. I lit a cigarette and relaxed before starting another session of the hot dusty work.

'Honey, I smelled your perfume sweetie this morning'…

20} "NO, YOU DIDN' T" ….

'Are you here sweetie?'…….

It was around eleven a.m. and getting extremely hot and humid even on the lower fourth floor.…

21} "HEY YOU TOOK A PISS YOU'RE A PIG"….

'Fourth floor, Thursday July twenty second a quarter after eleven in the morning… Is there a ghost on the fourth floor? … If you are here say something… Are you the shadow?.... Have you savages been working here?'.

'Walking the mile… Walking the long mile'………

'Hey you guys, I took a de wormer last night I'm feeling good, feeling better. That's why I now wear this mask all the time'....

22} "SEE HOW HIS BODY WORKS"...

23} "LOOK BACK"....................

'Brutal, I said as I cleared my throat of all the dust. Almost lunch time twenty minutes'….. The second best part of the day'.

I took another break pouring water onto my arms, back and chest…

I swept the floors in a few of the rooms then went down the grey striped stairwell for my lunch …

24} "OH SHUT UP"… "WHY SHOULD I?"…"SHUT UP"

I finished my lunch break and made my way back to the tower where Silvio was rinsing off with the water hose just inside the back doors on the wall. We talked a few minutes about the small amount of asbestos in the building and how it would be removed later on in the project.

25} "I'M HERE TO F*#K WITH YOU"…

'You know what I took last night, I asked him. Before I went to bed I took some de wormer pills. Do you know what that is?' I asked, as he looked up. 'In case you have parasites you take the pills and next morning you go to the washroom and get rid of anything that was in your system. I woke up this morning Silvio feeling much better. I recommend it if you are feeling ill from working in here'.

He chuckled as he mentioned he was okay.

I took the purple striped stairwell back up to the fourth floor.

'De wormer purple striped stairwell ghoulies'…

I walked up the few flights of stairs to the fourth floor landing ….

26} "BE CERTAIN"………. "NO PROBLEM"….

I prepared to start my afternoon first calling Tina at work.

She asked if I had decided to perform the cleansing on the building to rid the tower of the evil spirits. It was something that freaked me out the more I thought about it.

I still wasn't sure if I wanted to do it.

Sweeping gave me plenty of quiet time to think of life in general. I would wait for God's okay before trying anything like that.

I finished the week intact and thoroughly enjoyed a nice weekend with Tina and some of our friends. I continued my audio recordings on Monday morning up on the fifth floor.

'I have to mark my territory again … What do you ghoulies think of that... Sorry guys but I can't always make it to the washroom downstairs…. Sorry sweetie and jackson but that's the way it is I guess…. Do you ghosts have to go to the washroom like us humans or what?'……………

27} "GET OUT"….

'So what did you freaks do this weekend? ….. Did you pray… Did you ask for forgiveness?'…….. 'Do you ghoulies make each other cry or what?'……

'Jackson is a ho bo…. jackson is a ho bo'….

28} "DUMB F*#KER"….

'Ghoulies ghoulies'… Alright fourth floor ghosts on the fourth floor'.

I sang a rendition of a Dr. Seuss™ song.

'You're a mean one mister grinch…… I wouldn't touch you jackson with a…. Ten and a half foot pole ba, ba, ba, ba, ba da'… I whistled out a chorus then added; 'K jackson and sweetie and all you other dozens and dozens of demons in here, I wouldn't touch you with a…. Twenty five and a half foot pole ba, ba, da, da, da, da, ba, da, da, da, da, da'.

I eventually heard Silvio from around the corner. He approached me and told me to gather the pipes on the sixth floor as well as hammer off any metal on the ceilings and scrap it. The poor guy was running around like crazy.

I was always aware that the ghosts would be around me at one point or another during the day. And no wonder; there were so many of them.

'What's up?', I asked the invisible airways. 'No worries ghoulies I will clean it for you'.

'Walking the mile, walking the grey mile'.

Tuesday morning I filmed the twenty fifth floor starting with the back elevator shaft room with the hole cut out of the doors. I knew from experience and the rumors that the ghosts at the Park Sets Motel tended to hang out in the shaft. Maybe they slept there at night when the building was quiet, literally just hanging or floating there, who really knew right? I hoped to get more faces staring out from the openings.

I already had a number of pictures of faces and eyes from different floors looking back out at me from the back rooms. One of the faces I captured in front of an elevator door I called Mr. Magoo™ because he looks so much like the cartoon character. After filming the back room I walked to my right showing the scenic view from one balcony to the next. 'Totally awesome', I said as I walked around to film the six balcony areas.

'I left that eagle a banana peel and tomato right on the edge of the railing there. Hopefully he will come around again', I said as I zoomed in on the meal.

I had yet to see the eagle again. It was a thrill having been so close to a large eagle twenty five floors up.

I walked to the purple striped stairwell landing, filmed it a moment and said; 'What's up guys?'... I shut the camera off and walked down to the twentieth floor. I finished the day looking forward to taking Friday off for an extra long four day weekend.

Tina and I were going up north to spend time with my brother Terry and his girlfriend Babette. We were going to a bluegrass festival and then Tina and I were planning to visit my fathers and sister's gravesites.

Wednesday morning I started another e.v.p. session.

'Wednesday July the twenty seventh or eighth I don't remember'…

29} "GET OUT"…

'Tenth floor.'

'Ghoulies ghoulies yeah, yeah, yeah, ghoulies, ghoulies, ha, ha, ha, ooh… I hate ghoulies…… What's up'……..

30} "DON'T LOOK AT ME"….

'Morning ghoulies'……

'Oh look at that cross on the wall there. Did you notice it?'….

I was still debating whether to drive them out of the tower. I decided to wait until my last day.

31} "SLOW DOWN"….

Finally it was Thursday morning. I was feeling content driving to work looking forward to the long weekend. As we hadn't spent a lot of time together over the years I was looking forward to getting to know my brother better and catch up on lost time.

Tina hadn't spent any time in the country so she was really looking forward to it. We needed the peace and serenity of leaving the city and waking up to barren nature instead of concrete.

I continued recording at seven a.m. I walked in through the side entrance and waited for the others at the elevator foyer.

'Good morning hooligan's'.

Silvio came around the corner.

'Good morning sir how are you buddy?'

'Morning I am good. Okay you ready'?

'I am ready man. I have some spies up there waiting for me. I have to be ready'.

'Today I am changing your schedule. What floor is your stuff '?

'Seven'.

We were going up to the seventeenth floor where he would show me what to do. We went back down to the seventh floor first.

'This place sure looks different with everything opened up. You have been here a long time, last year maybe'? I asked Silvio.

'No just since February'.

'Oh I thought you guys did the top floors, but I remember now what you told me about the last company getting caught stealing, and then Hector took over right?'…

32} "MARF"… "KEEP THEM"…

'That's right'.

We arrived on the seventh floor.

'Yeah I'm just going to grab my little ladder'.

'Yeah I have a ladder if you need it too unless it is too big', he said.

'I like my little baby'.

'I don't know if you can reach you might have to jump', Silvio replied.

'Oh come on we are tall like mountains man'.

He laughed at that and said; 'I'm not short it's the world that's too big'.

We took the elevator to the work floor. He let me out on seventeen.

33} "DON'T KILL HIM"….. "HE'S BROKEN, THE LAW"

I was to start hammering down the plaster from the ceiling in front of the elevators. First I went around and opened all the windows then prepared my mask and tools for the day. I placed my recorder in a hole in the wall and pressed record.

'Grey striped stairwell seventeenth floor and it's a mess. Do you know that Dace and Dario are not here? ….. Are you going to miss them?'…..

I set my small ladder up and started at one end of the foyer ceiling. It was easy work but sometimes loose plaster would go down my shirt and pants. It got better as I went along and got used to it. It was a great workout though and I took as many short breaks as I thought my body needed. I went to my truck at morning break then took the purple striped stairwell stairs back up.

34} "WHO ARE YOU MEN" …. …………….. "LET ME KNOW" …

It was always an exhausting walk. This place was really wearing me out, I couldn't wait really to be finished with this haunted hell hole. I had had enough and my body needed a good rest.

35} "MOST STUBBORN HUNCHBACK"…

When lunch break was over I decided to bring up what I needed so I could stay up there for the rest of the day. I took my camera up too. I couldn't wait for the long weekend. It should be a great time and the weather would be nice. While pounding the ceiling I heard my phone chime letting me know I had a text message waiting.

I went to my phone and checked. It was from Tina so I took a break and called her back.

'Hello sweetheart.….. Walking in the hallway…….

36} "I'M HERE, TURN AROUND AND FIGHT"…..

Uh huh … That's right……. To what?……… Alright…… Oh well….. As long as everyone is ready….. We can put that in the back……All right anyways I'm almost done … Thank God its been a good day and I'm looking forward to coming home. Ill let Silvio know that my sister needs my help and I can't work tomorrow. Thanks for calling sweetheart, alright see you soon bye'.

It was close to afternoon break as I called my mechanic to book an appointment for Tina's car.

'Fine Steve and how are you buddy…. Oh good me too man…. Oh well as long as everything is okay….. Good, good…… I'm far away from home too; I'm at the haunted motel………. You're in Quebec… Well I hope you're having a good time…. It's good you're getting an extra long weekend glad to hear that. I'll give Nate a call if he is at the office, I just wanted to bring barney in; I noticed the check engine light………. Yeah the escort…… No that's forest……. forest and barney yeah'.

We laughed at the irony. We had known each other a long time.

'I'd like to drop it off on Tuesday night and just leave it there………. 97 escort……….. That's okay I'm on break here on the fifteenth floor just looking at the scenery…. And your where in Quebec?.... Okay I'll look that up on line……. Share the memories then back to work eh…. Be careful… Talk to you later thanks mate, bye'.

'Silvio', I bellowed through a hole below me. He didn't answer. I closed the windows, hid the tools and gathered my things, taking the grey striped stairwell stairs to the main floor. I turned the video camera on and filmed the old activity games room with all the contents from the rooms stored inside. I filmed the children's play room crammed full with the old out dated beautiful artifacts. And I filmed the once busy passenger elevator foyer. I filmed the grey striped stairwell. I shut the camera off as Silvio came out of the elevator.

'Sorry about not working tomorrow. Monday is a holiday so I hope you have some fun'.

'I'll try, see you Tuesday', he said.

'Thanks Silvio have a good weekend'.

I walked out to the truck and felt a weight lift off my shoulders. I was ready to relax and enjoy my life this weekend with all its blessings, adventures and memories, come what may. I left the haunted tower knowing that the mysterious spirits would be here when I returned.

1} masculine-voice 2} feminine-whisper 3} masculine-voice 4} masculine-voice 5} masculine-whisper 6} masculine-voice 7} feminine-voice 8} feminine-little girl voice 9} masculine-voice 10} masculine-voice 11} masculine-voice, feminine-voice 12} masculine-voices 13} masculine-voice 14} masculine-voice 15} masculine-voice 16} masculine-voice 17} masculine-voice 18} masculine-voice 19} masculine-voice 20} masculine-voice 21} masculine-voice 22} masculine-voice 23} masculine-voice 24} masculine-voices 25} masculine-voice 26} masculine-voices 27} masculine-voice 28} masculine-voice 29} masculine-voice 30} masculine-voice 31} masculine-whisper 32} masculine-voices 33} feminine-voice, masculine-voice 34} masculine-voices 35} masculine-voice 36} masculine-voice.

One of my favorites. I called him Mr. Magoo.™ Face in brown doorway, left side edge of photo.

A couple of beasts hanging out in the back elevator shaft.

↑↑↑↑↑↑

Picture from inside of elevator # 3, leading out onto one of the floors. How many ghoulies can you find? I see at least seven including the bald one near the top right corner. They liked to keep me company in the elevators.

Chapter Eleven; This Ain't Like Heaven

Jude 6 ***And the angels which kept not their first estate, but left their own habitation, he hath reserved in everlasting chains under darkness unto the judgement of the great day.***

I felt refreshed and rested after returning from my brother's serene rural retreat and I had been able to get re acquainted with my family roots. Tina and I had spent time at my brother's trailer park. We attended a blue grass festival being held there for the long weekend. We actually helped with security being part of a team making sure nobody brought any glass containers or beer bottles into the park. We had a good time. It was great spending time with my only brother. He had just released an instrumental bluegrass music c d, so I was able to purchase some copies.

On Sunday Tina and I left the festival and drove to North Bay to visit a museum, and then we drove to the two scarcely populated towns to the cemeteries where my father, three of my sisters and other relatives were buried. I hadn't been there for many years and for some reason we couldn't find my sisters grave markers at the cemetery. We spent a few hours in the area including driving to where my grandparents, my father's parent's old farm house used to stand on the road named after them, Carriere Rd.

On our way home we stopped to visit one of my Aunts and Uncles at their trailer park. My Aunt was playing guitar and singing for a small group that was gathered. It was nice to sit and enjoy the music and camaraderie of the visit. I had a chance to talk with my Uncle who I hadn't seen in many years. We drove home on Sunday evening almost running out of gas finding an open gas station off of the highway just in time. The truck was literally running on fumes. I vowed not to let that happen again to Tina's great relief. We were back home early enough and we still had tomorrow to enjoy the last day of the long weekend.

Waking up Tuesday morning for work I knew it wouldn't be long before my days working at the monstrous tower were over, so I was determined to inspire as many ghosts to talk as I could. I started my e.v.p. work shortly after the morning break.

'Tuesday August third, fourteenth floor almost done. I'm going to sing you ghosts a nice tune' I said as I whistled a rendition of a song.

It was Billy Joel's song, The Stranger. I whistled out part of the song. It sounded pretty good if I do say so.

'Yeah we all have a face that we hide away forever, and we only take it out, when no one is around.'

I hummed the parts that I couldn't remember as I gathered the debris. I walked around the floor checking on what was left to do.

1} "KEEP UP THE FAITH"...

I walked back to the front elevator foyer to start hammering the plaster from the ceiling. First I took the small light bulbs out of their sockets.

'Practice my baseball', I said, smashing them against the wall to my invisible back catcher. Some were strikes. Next I dislodged the light fixtures and cut the cords. I hummed the tune to William Tells Overture ….

2} "SCARY SITUATION"

I took a short break around ten thirty. In the dead quiet I crowed like a crow three times; 'Caw, caw, caw…

3} "GET OUT"…

'Dario and Dace are back ghoulies… What do you think of that? They're back'…

I resumed recording right after lunch as I waited in the foyer for the elevator. They were both working at the time so I took one up.

'I'm in front of the twelfth floor elevator…. Fun wow………… I'm tired of working here guys…. Hard on the body but how would you guys know…… But I can do all things through Christ who strengthens me… Just telling you…………

4} "DOES GOD LOVE YOU?"….

5} "GHOSTS, WE AREN'T"…

Wherever I left my recorder, whether it was in my pocket, on a ledge or a crevice or hole, it always managed to record voices and whispers that were not human. I picked up some odds and ends from the floor and tossed them into piles as I whistled a rendition of Amazing Grace……..

6} "TOO BAD"…

I made it to the tenth floor out of breath and finished the day pounding the plaster off of the ceiling.

Wednesday morning was another hot one in August; the dog days of summer whatever that really means. I started the recorder when I finished opening the windows. My phone rang. It was Silvio. I told him I was on the tenth floor. He was coming up to see me so I waited in front of the elevator and I could slightly hear the wind in the shaft and the elevator moving up, then down.

'Stuck on the tenth floor'…. I whistled a short tune while waiting …

7} "DA, DA, DA" …

My phone rang again. It was Silvio. There was something wrong with the elevator again so I climbed the stairs to nineteen where Silvio wanted me to work with a welder who had been called in to cut the remaining pipe running vertically from top to bottom beside the back elevator shafts in the back rooms. I waited in the coolest spot by the back room. The welder walked around the corner and towards me. He said he had been waiting half an hour downstairs so he took the stairs instead.

'Oh I know. I had to take the stairs too. I'm sweating already doing nothing.'

8} "THAT'S SWEAT THERE" …

He said his name was Carter. He explained what I would be doing to help him to cut the pipes down. We walked back to the back service room and he started cutting the pipe as I stood back and took it easy.

I was feeling discouraged having found that my last pay cheque had bounced, a big amount about sixteen hundred dollars. The company was replacing it but it made me feel un appreciated. I had to wait five days for the replacement cheque to clear my bank. Who ever said life was always perfect or fair?

It was hot working around the torches, almost unbearable actually and noisy when the cut pipe would fall onto the concrete floor. All in all the work went well.

I drove to the coffee shop then took my time driving back enjoying the rest. I carried my java upstairs and finished my break in the gloomy tower. The morning passed by a little too boring and twelve o'clock came slower than usual. I enjoyed the air conditioning in the truck again and thoroughly devoured the awesome lunch Tina had prepared for me. She is a blessing in my life. One way I thanked her for her love was by giving her my pay.

As I relaxed I wondered how many people could have handled hearing voices and seeing images from the other side. She was probably braver than I was in these matters and truly supported me through the haunting.

I finished my lunch and waited with Carter for the elevator.

'This is an old building though huh?', he asked.

'Nineteen sixty-nine, I answered. It is a strong building.'

'I heard people talking saying something about a while back some people were killed in this building'.

'Yes they died in a fire in nineteen seventy eight'.

Someone had to operate the one working elevator non stop or it would get stuck so Silvio took over. The doors opened and we went up to the ninth floor. By two fifteen in the afternoon I was back at hammering the plaster from the elevator foyer, now on the seventh floor. I finished it by break time. During the afternoon I took a brief video of the fourth floor.

Next I filmed the front elevator foyer. All three of the passenger elevators were out of service. Elevator # 3 was sitting stuck with the doors opened on the fourth floor. Good thing it got stuck with the doors open and not closed with someone inside. The fire dept. would have had to have been called in for the rescue for sure. Scary stuff indeed.

After my break I started the sixth floor. Every now and then a bell would ring from the elevator. They were trying to fix it. Silvio walked by just in front of me scaring me as usual, cackling his famous laugh as he did.

At one point while pounding the ceiling with the side of a hammer, I instinctively spun around on my ladder sensing that something was behind me. I just knew there had been. I could feel the negative energy. I wasn't being paranoid and I knew that for certain as it was the only time in six months that I felt the need to defend myself in that way.

9} "WE DON'T LIKE YOU"…

I walked around to a few of the windows soaking up the sun and spectacular view. I felt content while driving home that afternoon knowing my time at the motel was almost over and that my body and mind could soon rest.

I drove to work that Thursday morning knowing that this was probably my last week working in the haunted motel. I arrived at work and took the grey striped stairwell to the seventh floor and waited for Carter to arrive. When he did we carried on with our routine from yesterday. Carter went in to the back room to start the cutting and I waited in the room just outside of it until he needed my help.

10} "WHAT'S UP? EVRYBODY HATES YOU"

Carter was on the fifth floor by nine am. I walked to the elevators to sweep debris away from the doors. Silvio was there with one of the new Cuban workers in the now fixed elevator, explaining how to operate it so he wouldn't get stuck. I knew from experience that getting into these elevators was a gamble as to whether you got out or not. I stood and listened while Silvio talked, and I eventually said;

'Make sure you tell him to have his cell phone with him just in case, so he can call his family and tell his wife he loves her'.

'Yeah and tell her he is going to miss her', Silvio added.

We both laughed, and I said to the worker;

'Don't worry you will be okay we'll pray for you'.

I went back and waited in the farthest room while Carter torched the pipes. I looked down one of the numerous smaller holes in the concrete to the next floor and noticed Silvio sitting at his desk doing paper work. I found a piece of blue nylon cord and used it to try to scare Silvio. I was right above him.

'Silvio,' I said slow and ghost like…

'Ooooooohhhhhhhhhh', he replied……

'Silvio', I said again……

'Ooooooohhhhhhhhhhh', he said back.

I lowered the string down through the hole till it was near his face……….

'Ooooooooooohhhhhhhhhhhhhh', he answered again in a spookier higher tone.

It was fun to kid around at work. Good thing Silvio had a sense of humour though.

I crouched down and enjoyed the quiet stillness of doing nothing.

During my break I listened to the news. Some lady had fallen from an eleventh floor balcony and a satellite dish had broken her fall. A man had apparently thrown her over and was facing an attempted murder charge. Craziness was everywhere. Who needed ghosts?

We finished with the pipes shortly after ten o'clock and Silvio had me go to the ninth floor to shovel up the plaster from the front foyer. I found jackson the shovel on the eighth floor and brought him to earn his pay. I shoveled all the loose debris together.

11} "HELP ME OUT OF HERE"….

Then I went down to the seventh floor to clean up that foyer. As I took a short break I heard the Cuban guy yelling.

'Hey'.

It sounded like near the elevators.

'Heeeyyyy'.

There it was again. I walked over to the foyer……

'Hey…. Hey, hey', I heard again.

The sound was below me so I went down the grey striped stairwell to the next floor as the elevator bell went off. I went to the elevator door and listened and heard it again …

'Hey'!

I knocked on the door and said; 'what floor are you on … what floor?'….

I heard a faint 'hey', and then Silvio trying to help the guy stuck in the elevator.

I wondered if he was calling his wife right about now. He might need a clean pair of shorts too. I heard him yell again as I went back up to the seventh floor. I hoped he was okay.

I wasn't hearing any more yelling or bells so I assumed he had spent about five minutes stuck in elevator number three which was the only one still working. Lucky guy.

I walked down to the third floor and talked with Silvio. He had no idea what had just happened but the elevator opened up and had let the guy out.

I walked down the purple striped stairwell singing; 'Ghoulies ghoulies hah, hah, hah, ghoulies, ghoulies rah, rah, rah; ooh I love ghoulies'.

12} "I KNOW IT, I KNOW"

I reached the main floor and walked out to have lunch in my truck.

My thoughts wandered as they often did thinking of whether tomorrow would be my last day here. I decided I would have no regrets, that fear or no fear God willing, I would do a cleansing of the tower to deal with the spirits to insist that they leave this gloomy tower of pain and misery so it might have a brighter future of peace and happiness.

1} feminine-whisper 2} masculine-voice 3} masculine-voice 4} masculine-whisper 5} masculine-voice 6} masculine-voice 7} masculine-voice 8} masculine-whisper 9} masculine-voice 10} masculine-voice 11} masculine-voice 12} masculine-voice.

That room on the second floor was always locked off so I don't know who or what that was staring at me as I sat in my truck. Weird looking, if it's human.

Chapter Twelve; The Darkness Fell

Luke 4: 8 **And Jesus answered and said unto him, Get thee behind me, Satan: for it is written, Thou shalt worship the Lord thy God, and him only shalt thou serve.**

As I drove into work on Friday morning I figured today would be my last at the haunted tower. It had been an interesting experience to say the least and one I never could have imagined would be so intense. I had decided I would attempt to drive the evil spirits out of the tower so they would not be able to scare or threaten anyone else, hopefully ever again.

Tina had come up with an idea. Last night she had recorded a short prayer on an extra recorder we had purchased. I wouldn't be doing it alone. Tina's recorded prayer to the spirits would be playing so they would hear her along with me insisting that they had to leave.

I arrived at work and walked through the big wooden doors at the back of the motel like so many times before, likely for the last time. I was sad but also felt a sense of relief. I would miss the interaction with the other side but felt relieved that I wouldn't have to deal with their aggression and insanity any longer. They had scared everyone who had worked in the tower during the renovation and I assumed other people had experienced their haunting routines throughout the years.

I walked past the back elevator shaft in the service bay area through another door and then turned right and walked up to the third floor using the grey striped stairwell. Silvio was in his room at the table sitting and doing the time sheets for the remaining workers. I hadn't seen Dace and Dario for most of the week. I was the last of the original crew still working in the old motel along with three Cuban workers hired for the last of the work.

'Good morning my friend'.

'Good morning Exi. Hector called me last night to tell me today is your lay off. Everything is almost finished in here.'

'I figured we wouldn't be here for much longer. Perfect timing really I'm worn out man. I don't know about you but I am looking forward to resting my body for a while. What should I do for today boss, just keep cutting and gathering the wire?'

'Yep just keep busy. The other guys are cleaning the plaster up'.

'Alrighty budge I will see you later. Have a good day', I said as I walked up to the fifth floor to start my last day.

It was a little cooler working in the tower compared to most mornings. The humidity had decreased somewhat. It was a good day to work. As I got into my routine my thoughts were on whether I would be brave enough to attempt the exorcism. I felt reserved about the thought of evicting the ghosts, but after all they were evil. I had to keep reminding myself of that. They had hurt people and had threatened and harassed. Deep down I had a hatred and disgust towards them.

They were sinister and they had to go. I knew I would feel worse if I did nothing, leaving them open opportunities to haunt and hurt the new residents. I hoped I could gather up the nerve to tell them to leave. I tried to convince myself that I wasn't afraid of the demon spirits and to just do it.

As the morning dragged on I knew I was afraid of the invisible world living in the massive tower. This was their territory too and I wondered if they would fight back some how. I felt less and less confident. Thinking about performing my first exorcism freaked me out to be totally honest. It was something I thought I would never be involved in. It was something someone else did, not me. I tried to stay focused on the work and took the day one minute at a time.

At break I went to my truck for my camera and recorder. I brought my lunch with me too, planning to stay in the tower at lunch time so I could venture upstairs and cleanse the building. I had a bottle of holy water that Tina had received from Jordan. I started the last e.v.p. session at eleven thirty in the morning.

'Walking the mile, walking the long mile for the last time', I said as I walked up to the fifth floor.

I definitely was not using the elevator on my last day here. I wasn't taking that chance. I opened the windows for some fresher air and took a break by an open window. I carried my small step ladder to the middle of a room and started cutting the red wire in the ceiling so it could be collected later.

1} "I KNOW YOU"…

I was feeling more and more anxious as lunch time approached. My plan was to walk to the top floor while everyone else would be outside of the building and then attempt the eviction. It creeped me out thinking about it but I decided I would just do it and get it over with. I was hoping I would have no regrets. If a demon lunged at me I would try and fight back. My mind was racing with different thoughts of all the various outcomes and consequences.

'Don't get yourself going' I told myself. Stay positive and be strong. Have faith in God's awesome power.

He had protected me this far, but fear was still a powerful human emotion. I sang an Elton John song; Captain Fantastic.

At lunch time I grabbed my personal belongings and walked to the sixth floor. I would wait until I knew the other workers were having lunch before going upstairs. I opened the windows and had a quick sandwich before getting up enough nerve to climb the creepy grey striped stairwell.

I was too nervous to climb the haunted purple striped one, where the seven people had died in the fire so many years ago.

'Friday August the sixth. I'm getting laid off today.'

I got my cell phone out and called Tina to let her know I was recording and starting the climb. I would call her when I reached the top floor.

I grabbed what I needed for the task and started the climb up the stairs. I was tired and afraid but climbed in faith.

'Thank you Jesus…. Praise God… Thank you Lord…… Too much stuff in my pockets…. Holy water of Jordan too, yeah, yeah, yeah………… Grey striped stairwell sixteenth floor… Nine to go. Going to twenty five', I said as

I took a minute break trying to catch my breath; 'Going to do battle with all you demons'…

I continued climbing in the hot oppressive stairwell.

'With the power of Jesus Christ and the protection of his blood…….. I command you all to gather on the twenty fifth floor in Jesus' name …….. By the power invested in me… By the mercy and faith in God and Christ…….

You will stay in the back elevator until I am ready… That's a direct command from the Holy Spirit and power from the resurrection'…….

I rambled on feeling somewhat fearful.

'I'm covered by his blood ….. In Jesus' name; 'They shall cast out demons and unclean spirits of every kind'…….

I reached the twenty fifth floor.

'Alright, here I come you spirits, demons from the pit of hell'.

I turned to my right passing the passenger elevators as I made my way towards the back elevator shaft room out of breath, my heart pounding and my legs feeling weak as I passed the purple striped stairwell. I reached the back room and turned on the camera setting it down to record a video of the cut out squares in and around the elevator door exposing the darkness of the shaft and the demon's favorite hang out. I adjusted the camera to the best position.

'There's a nail on the floor similar to the nail that Jesus Christ was nailed to the cross with. …….. Amen……. Amen'…

I stood between the camera and the exposed shaft making sure the audio recorder of Tina's prayer was ready to play. I called Tina from my phone.

'Hi babe here we go.….. The holy water bottle was empty. It must have evaporated or something but I filled it with bottled water so that should be okay, here we go. Enjoy the show, hang on.'

I turned on Tina's recorded prayer as I opened the blessed water and began sprinkling drops of it in and around the elevator shaft openings.

'Amen', I said as I tried to think of what to say. 'Thank you Jesus….. You ghosts are commanded to depart from this building forever….. There will be no more hauntings; you will go wherever God wants you to go. Thank you Lord…. Amen….. Good riddance……… Thank you for the resurrection and the power and protection of your blood, your glory and might…….. I believe in God the Father maker of heaven and earth…. Amen……. Me and my beautiful wife Tina……. Wherever God wants you to go it is done ……. Amen'….

I turned off Tina's recorded voice as we spoke on the phone.

'Alright……… That was easy……….. I gotta go……… Ciao, love you'.

I walked back toward the purple striped stairwell.

'Ah, this place feels good, feels cleaner….. Alright it's an improvement praise God….. Thank you Jesus.'

I started my descent down the purple striped stairwell.

'That was easy…. That was real easy.'

I was glad it was done. I had performed the cleansing. Tina and I with the Lords powerful Spirit.

I hummed a song as I descended the last of the stairs. I felt lighter with more energy. 'Alright awesome…. This building is clean. The next people are safe'.

I was back on the sixth floor and walked over to my things on the ledge.

'It even smells better in here.'

I took another short break feeling good about what I had just done. I wondered if it had worked. It did feel better all of a sudden, much less oppressive than I was used to. The air felt lighter, cleaner. I sat by the open window.

'It feels so good not to have demons around me. That's awesome. Awesome!….. I don't know what took me so long….I had to learn and increase my faith. Thank you Jesus'.

It was almost one o'clock and I was looking forward to the end of this day and the freedom from working in this building. One hour to go.

My spirit had gone through many struggles in dealing with this haunting and I would leave this place wiser and stronger in the knowledge of knowing I had stuck with it and had risen above the evil that I had been exposed to.

At two o'clock I gathered my things and brought the tools to the third floor. There leaning against a wall was my old friend jackson, the big plastic shovel. It had helped me do a lot of work in this massive structure. I noticed Silvio coming around the corner. I held my hand out to shake his.

'Well my friend we did it. We got through the hard work and the ghosts didn't get the best of us either'.

'Yeah almost finished. I will be here maybe for a few more days', he said.

'Oh, well you be careful. You shouldn't have any more trouble with the ghosts. I believe they are gone', I replied. It sure was an interesting experience for me. You are a good boss and a great guy Silvio. It was a pleasure working with you', I said as I shook his hand again.

'I'll give you a call in the next few weeks if you would still like to come by, maybe on a weekend. It would be great having you over'.

'Sure man, he said. Just give me a call that sounds good Exi'.

'Okay my friend I will call you for sure. Thanks for everything Silvio. All bosses should be as cool as you'.

He laughed; 'Thanks man. You're alright too. You did a good job in this place.'

'Hey Silvio can I ask you one more thing? Can I have jackson for a souvenir'?

'Sure why not. Someone broke your ladder, so I don't mind it is only fair'.

'Thanks that's cool having this memento of this job. I'll talk with you soon buddy'.

I grabbed jackson and walked down the winding hall that led to the side entrance, the hall where I first smelled perfume not so long ago. I walked outside hoping I had somehow made a difference. And I knew that working at this old haunted motel had changed me in profound ways, some that would follow me like dark shadows.

Changes that I could use with fear or use with courage to deal with anything strange or dangerous.

I vowed to come back and visit during the open house a few years from now. Yes, God willing I'd be back to visit the sleeping giant.

Maybe I will be reminded of the past with the smell of sweetie's perfume. One thing the haunting has definitely taught me is that you just never know if you are really completely alone.

1} masculine-voice

↑ ↑

'You will stay in the back elevator until I am ready'.
James 2: 19 **Thou believest that there is one God; thou doest well; the devils also believe and tremble.**

A picture of the bottle of holy water I used to perform the cleansing of the motel. Also the small wooden cross I always wore fastened to my front shirt pocket.

The back of one of my work T-shirts that I painted with semi-gloss paint. Notice how the cross section looks a lot like the face of the Shroud of Turin. This shirt must have freaked the demons out.

Last but not least a picture of my helper jackson.

Chapter Thirteen; The Things In Between

> 1 John 4: 1-6 *¹Beloved, believe not every spirit, but try the spirits whether they are of God: because many false prophets are gone out into the world. ²Hereby know ye the Spirit of God: Every spirit that confesseth that Jesus Christ is come in the flesh is of God: ³And every spirit that confesseth not that Jesus Christ is come in the flesh is not of God: and this is that spirit of antichrist, whereof ye have heard that it should come; and even now already is it in the world. ⁴Ye are of God, little children, and have overcome them: because greater is he that is in you, than he that is in the world. ⁵They are of the world: therefore speak they of the world, and the world heareth them. ⁶We are of God: he that knoweth God heareth us; he that is not of God heareth not us. Hereby know we the spirit of truth, and the spirit of error.*

It never fails to amaze me at how the bizarre things that happen in our lives might have something to do with invisible forces or entities that we usually don't realize are affecting our reality, no matter how big those distractions might be. I know my experience with the haunting at the grand towering motel has changed me but I'm still not sure exactly how. I'm assuming if you have read this far into the book it has interested you and hopefully you believe that I have told the truth to the best of my ability. Looking back on it now, I realize it was an insane nerve racking adventure that I allowed myself to be a part of.

I believe that some of our life involves looking back and trying to put the mysterious pieces of events that have occurred in our lives together, so that as time goes by they make more sense somehow.

I could have ignored the scary demons. But right from the first white blob captured on video I knew I couldn't ignore them. I was fascinated by them. They were hanging around scaring everybody and looking back now that it's over, I don't think I could have functioned very well if I had tried to ignore the evil. I would have quit. I know that now for sure.

I was innocently shooting a video to show my wife the fantastic view from a higher floor in an old worn out motel and was introduced to another world. Mankind is instinctively curious. The more curious I was about something being there the more passionate I was about finding it. I allowed it to draw me to itself like the mystery it was.

Prayers do get answered so my advice is be careful for what is hoped for. This nightmarish experience exposed its existence to me and caught me by surprise. My advice to anyone exposed to the spirit world would be to make sure that you know what you believe in, and why you believe it. I have learned that challenging and confronting the spirit world involves using the authority and might that comes from above, some strategy, and what some people choose to call luck as well.

One of my motives for writing this book is to expose that much more the invisible entities that exist all around us. There will always be skeptics. I know I will probably never fully know why I was introduced to these spirit beings, but I was. Hopefully I can tell my children about it. It's proven to be the most bizarre experience of my life.

I have heard that once a person is attacked by a spirit he or she can remain a target. That speculative theory is being played out.

I have saved this chapter as a compilation of recorded activity away from work that was recorded during and after my encounters at the motel. I think it's important that you are made aware that spirits are everywhere and can and do follow us around if they want to.

We are generally not aware of them because we are involved in our own everyday visible logical lives. They are intelligent and probably understand more languages than most people do. They hear us and understand us and can view us as potential victims of their insane world. Maybe they have to engage with us and maybe they don't, but they do.

And they use fear as their number one weapon to intimidate us and to make us believe we are the crazy ones.

The following pages are also fact based recorded experiences that Tina and I have encountered on different occasions.

The first encounter with the other side was on an August long weekend when Tina and I visited a tour of a museum in northern Ontario Canada, on a Sunday afternoon.

As I videoed the tour with permission, an employee of the museum guided us with information about the Dionne Quintuplet Museum.

'In 1925 the house was purchased by the father. Their mother was twenty five years old when they were born and she already had five other children'.

We walked from room to room starting in the small bedroom with the double bed and an old incubator in the corner that was used for the five babies. It was the first incubator in Canada back in 1934. The house was old, a two storey building maybe five hundred square feet in size. The original walls were painted in a yellow eggshell color.

'So I'll let you look around, if you have any questions let me know'.

I focused the camera on the numerous pictures on the walls. The quints were very famous back then; phenomena for the time. I zoomed in on a picture of a man with the five infants and asked the guide; 'So that's the father down here?'

'Yes that's their father there and that's one of the nurses with the girls'....

1} "GO CHECK ON THE GIRLS"....

'Just look at how tiny they are eh Exi', Tina said.

The tour guide went on to tell us that two of the nurses had delivered the first three quints and then the doctor arrived and delivered the last two. When the quints were about a month old their father sold their names to The Chicago Worlds Fair™, being worried with no money. He didn't know what else he could do to take care of five more children all at one time.

Years later the government stepped in to stop the exploitation of the girls.

'Is there an upstairs'? I asked her.

'There was an upstairs to the home at one time and there would have been three bedrooms but it's closed off right now', she said.

'Has there ever been any hauntings, people dying or anything like that?' I asked.

'No nothing like that. A psychic came in one time and said that one of the nurses was still in here, but'.

'Yeah right, I said. Maybe she misses the place.'

A few more people came in for a tour.

'Thanks so much', I said.

'Oh no problem'.

Tina and I looked around the room at the furniture, among them the old expensive dining room table given as a wedding gift, and then we walked into a small room where the girl's different outfits were displayed behind glass.

'So nurse are you still here or what, I asked. You must miss the place it was an important part of your life after all'.

I videoed the different displays.

'Look at the little house coats', I said to Tina.

'That's like their handwriting up there too eh', Tina said …

2} "DON'T KNOW"…

We finished looking around and drove off.

That afternoon we made our way to my father's grave stone further north about half an hour away. I hadn't visited my father's burial ground for twenty years. It was a good way to reach back in time and try and feel a little closer to his memory. I recorded a short session at my father's grave stone. I lit a cigarette and spoke out into the invisible air.

'Yeah I'm still misbehaving dad I'm still smoking… But you know me, at least I care'…

3} "I KNOW THAT YOU CARE SON"...

   After walking through the cemetery we drove about a half hour further north to visit my deceased sisters and other relatives; my grandparents; [my mother's parents] and other extended family that I had never known. We did e.v.p. work and videoed for about an hour off and on but didn't catch anything else out of the ordinary. We drove back home that night and had the holiday Monday to relax.

   Six weeks or so after working at the motel Tina and I went back to the park across from the old motel to relax in the sun and do some more recording. Tina started an e.v.p. session.

   'Okay, September, twenty-fifth 2008 …

4} "GIL'S BACK"...

   … in the park across from the Park Sets Motel…. Weird ghoulie area….. So if you have anything to say speak now'...

   Tina has such a cute voice. It's one of many reasons I married her. I un wrapped my sandwich as Tina ate her soup.

   'Enjoying my yummy hot chicken noodle soup'….

   We sat awhile eating looking across to the huge concrete tower.

   'So you knuckleheads glad to see me?', I asked.

   'You guys remember my voice?', Tina asked.

   'Remember being evicted?', I said.

   We finished our lunch and as a plane flew overhead Tina asked;

   'So has any satanic ritual taken place in this area?... Any witchcraft or voodoo?...

5} "HA, HA, HA, HA, HA, HA"……..

'Looking forward to Halloween I guess eh schleps?' I said ….

"F*#K YOU GIL CARRIERE"……………….

'Where you guys living now?' I said…….. Anybody invite you back?'…….

6} "NO"….

The next recording session was on October 31st. Tina and I went back to the park across from the motel tower. We figured Halloween might be one of the more active times for spirit activity so we drove out there and spent a couple of hours enjoying the day and recording. We asked a lot of questions, really good ones. We were on a roll and kept the recorder going but didn't pick up a single whisper or voice. Maybe ghosts are too busy that time of year. Maybe they decided to ignore us for whatever reason. I was quite surprised that no activity was recorded.

'I'm writing a book about you guys what do you think of that?' I asked.

Not a peep. Oh well at least I had let them know.

The last session is the strangest of them all and one of my favorites. I had gone to visit my brother in Midland Ontario so we could talk over some of our mother's legal affairs. He was renting a basement apartment while working as a teacher. The owners of the house were friends and fellow teachers of his.

I had met them both. A nice couple. She had mentioned to me on my last visit as I was showing my brother some photos of the ghosts at the motel, that there was a ghost in her house. During a visit in November my brother was taking care of their small dog while they had to be out of town. I climbed the stairs from my brother's basement apartment with my recorder running. He was feeding the dog on the main floor.

It was a beautifully decorated home with nice styling and stained wood. Very comfortable.

'Any ghosts here?', I said walking up the stairs towards the kitchen where my brother Terry was scooping out dog food.

'There's the bro feeding the dog'.

'Hey Tina how are you doing,' he said noticing the camera.

'Hey Kali come here, come here Kali. She's too hungry she doesn't want to see me. It's really nice up here Terry'.

'Oh yeah, he said. They've fixed it up nice. There's a loft up there too'.

He went into the living room where I followed.

'See lately Terry I mean obviously you saw, you did see ghosts in my haunted motel I worked at right?'

'Well I didn't notice them as such but I saw I think one irregularity that looked like a little girl or something like that. That one there kind of freaked me a little bit. But I can't say I saw anything else.'

I wasn't quite sure what my brother really thought of ghosts. He didn't talk with me that much about it. We talked about the nicely renovated kitchen while he finished feeding the dog. It was always good to spend time with my only brother. He went into the living room and realized he had left his glass outside so he went out the sliding door to the deck. Kali the dog was almost finished eating.

'Come on I said, finish eating. Look you dropped one, here eat that'.

She was happy and started bouncing around; a small poodle by the way.

'What do you see a ghost huh? Show me where the ghost is. Hey Kali, Kali. Show me where the ghost is in Jesus' name come on, come and show me where the ghosty is.'

My brother came back in.

'You going out go ahead, he told her. No I guess not'.

He shut the sliding door.

'Who plays the tuba', I asked him, noticing one hanging on the wall.

'Ah I'm not sure.'….

7} "I DO" …

'I guess that's a trumpet, trumpet or a tuba', I said ……

8} "WA"….

'That's a tuba', Terry said.

'Tuba I was right.'….

9} "WA, WA"… "WA, WA, WA, WA AH"….. "WA, WA AH" …..

…..'Yeah probably eh, Terry said; but that's when they got married. They were in Italy I think'.

The conversation my brother and I were having was interrupted by that ghost's rendition of a tuba.

After reviewing the tuba playing recording I decided I wouldn't tell my brother about it until I knew that he had moved. I'm looking forward to him knowing about it if he wants to hear it.

__ The stories in this chapter are strange but true. All of the feminine and masculine whispers and voices recorded in this book are strange but true.

I could understand ghosts or demons haunting me at the sad old motel. They were there long before I got there but I didn't think they would follow me around when the job was finished.

Tina and I plan to go back and visit my old friend the grand tower during the open house not too long from now. I wonder if there will be any spirits roaming its floors. If there are my recorder will be their audience. But I believe the renovated tower will be full of peace and promise.

She is a strong structure. Now more than ever I solidly believe and truly know that we humans are surrounded by the spirit world everyday. Some are good, and some are bad. They have made my life more interesting and have awakened my spirit man in ways that I am still learning.

I plan to keep sharing this insane somewhere in the middle type of reality with others so that the truth can lead to freedom. I have heard that regret, anger and fear may attract unknown and unwanted entities. I have learned from experience, that saying is probably true.

1} feminine-voice 2} masculine-whisper 3} masculine-whisper 4} masculine-voice 5} masculine-whispers 6} masculine-whisper 7} masculine-voice 8} masculine-voice 9} masculine-voice

↑

De bunked this round headed looking goblin. Turned out to be a part of the railing reflecting off of the light.

↑

De bunked this spooky looking white head. Actually it is a lone white stone on the wall. It sure looked creepy though. Things are not always the way they seem to be in life.

Chapter Fourteen; Things That I've Seen

(One Year Later)

Mark 16: 17 ***And these signs shall follow them that believe; In my name shall they cast out devils……***

As I tried to fall asleep from another mentally and spiritually oppressive day, my thoughts and prayers went out to Almighty God along with the myriad number of prayers and petitions being sent by so many other people.

My spirit was grieved and weak. I was trying not to feel too discouraged with the ongoing situations in my life. It wasn't bad enough that I couldn't breathe well enough to be able to rest and hold down a job, I was still being tormented by the suffocating spirit and God knew what else because I didn't.

As I drifted into an uncomfortable sleep worrying about my breathing I noticed it was almost 1 am. I woke up suddenly, choking for air. As I calmed my fear I looked at the clock; 2:10 a.m.

That's it I thought angrily. I had to keep trying to get rid of whatever was attacking me. I was feeling drained but determined to use more authority to get the entities to tell me what their names were. So far they had been elusive. They wouldn't tell me their names or what right they had to be oppressing me.

Tonight I felt different. I was more determined than ever, and holding back tears of fear and frustration I got out of bed quietly so as not to wake Tina. I wanted her to get some rest from all the crazy oppression I had been going through. I knew I could and had to handle this on my own along with God's guidance and power.

'I can do all things through Christ which strengtheneth me', [Philippians Ch. 4:13]

I repeated this scripture verse to myself as I went into the den depressed then knelt down and prayed.

I read some of the bible for a while. I didn't quite know what I was doing but I needed to be close to God and His guidance. He seemed to want me to see them for some reason. I had the conviction to go to the washroom, look in the mirror and confront the spirits.

I opened up my little white King James Version of the bible I've had for many years. I started reading from it out loud while looking in the mirror addressing any spirit that might be present. I commanded in the name of Jesus a number of times for any evil spirit to come forth and tell me its name and what right it had to be in me.

Eventually by prayer and supplication by reading scripture out loud with the authority I had as a believer in Christ covered by His blood, they came out. Five of them. One by one. Like little piggies leaving the market.

The first one was a;

'Deaf and dumb spirit.'

And it told me so in a mumbled voice. As I looked in the mirror my eyes drooped then opened and closed a number of times while my lips pursed and my tongue flopped around lazily as the demon tried to talk. That lasted for about five minutes. As I slowly took control I cast it out in Jesus' name.

Getting my composure back I read more scripture, relieved that the authority and faith in Christ was sufficient for the spirits to answer and be in subjection to Him through me as His vessel.

I asked if there were any more demons present and to identify themselves.

The second one eventually came through saying it was;

'The spirit of rock and roll.'

And 'it' was cast out easier, quicker and more subtle than the first.

The third one to introduce itself said;

'I am a crow spirit'.

I was surprised at first but then I realized and remembered how me and a co-worker had 'cawed' three times like crows one day while working at the haunted motel.

This demon literally made my eyes bulge out like a crow and then left. It didn't caw though thank goodness.

The fourth spirit to manifest was a spirit I had totally forgotten about. It said in a deep voice;

'I am an old native spirit'.

As I stared at myself in the mirror, my face and eyes wrinkled up as an old shaman spirit came forth to reveal itself.

My spirit instinctly knew it was when I had ignorantly opened myself up to an old friend I used to smoke with. In exchange for the weed and my hospitality of food and sometimes a place to sleep for the night, my gypsy friend Nick would read my fortune with his tarot cards. That was over fifteen years ago. He was eccentric, friendly and a so called wise man who used to sleep outdoors and in trees and live as a free spirit. I had totally forgotten about those occultic experiences. I cast the spirit out in Jesus' name and my face returned to normal. I renounced my past occultic involvement with Nick.

The final demon to reveal itself identified itself as a;

'Most stubborn hunchback spirit'.

It entered me over a year ago while I was working at the Park Sets Motel. It was a very surreal feeling as I recalled numbing out one night after work. I had thought back then of the possibility of one of the ghosts from the motel getting inside of me somehow.

But back then I thought it was just my crazy imagination at play. I guess I was wrong, I looked at myself in the mirror and cast out the hunchback spirit, 'its' voice mimicking exactly the one I had recorded last year in the haunted dwelling.

I asked any more spirits to come forward but none did. I washed my face in disbelief, but in relief knowing in my spirit and my mind that I felt cleaner,

I could sense that I felt lighter and through Christ's awesome power, authority and mercy, I was breathing normally.

I slowly made a cup of tea thanking God quietly, so grateful that his love and guidance had guided me through a successful deliverance. I checked on Tina. She was still sleeping peacefully. I drank my tea and read more scripture from the gospel of Matthew.

I bowed my knee in prayer before going back to bed. I slept peacefully that night. It was 4:30 a.m. before I drifted off. I didn't wake up until 3:00 p.m. the next afternoon and I was still feeling worn out from the oppressive but successful battle I had won through the power of Jesus Christ.

As I wound down that evening I thought of how much more peace I felt compared to the last six weeks or so since the initial spiritual attack on my throat. Tina had commented earlier in the evening how it made sense to her that a suffocating spirit had been responsible for so much trouble lately considering the motel had suffered that fire and people had died of smoke inhalation, suffocating the victims to death. It made perfect sense. Very sad but true. They followed me home.

I fell asleep that night with no suffocating feeling for the first time in almost two months. It felt like I had been released from a prison sentence once held in bondage, now set free early maybe for good behavior and obedience.

I received spiritual confirmation as I sang a song of worship in the shower that night that God wanted us to go up north in the morning. I remember waking up a few times that night more out of habit than anything else and realizing I was okay, then falling back asleep, confident that God had provided for me once again. I realized I deserved the pit of hell but was delivered out of the grasp of the enemy of my soul by His mercy and grace once again.

My small amount of faith was growing day by day. I sensed that my spiritual battles weren't over but I knew I was winning over Satan's power and his innumerable demon helpers. The Holy Spirit was leading me into all righteousness, as long as I wanted to.

Early the next morning Tina and I left for my brother's trailer park up north far away from the rat race of the big city, a much needed break from the oppression of the last while. It was the bluegrass festival again just like last year except this time I would not be partying. I would have a few drinks, but I was concerned for my brother. There was a lot of drinking at the park and festival. I care for my family and for their salvation through Jesus Christ. I had been praying years for his conversion even as I had back slid as a Christian. I hoped that this time I would set a better example. I missed spending time with him.

It was a nice relaxing trip and I was happy Tina was getting a break from the bustle of work. She loved it in the country and I realized more and more that I loved her more than ever.

We arrived around two p.m. on Saturday and relaxed with my brother Terry and his girlfriend Babette and with some of her family and their friends on the porch of their trailer which faced a beautiful clean moving river as part of the front yard. It was truly a serene feeling and a breathtaking site; so tranquil and free.

That evening we got the chance to listen to one of my brother's favorite bands; he was telling me about the pros and cons of the music business; him being an awesomely talented musician. I was impressed and proud of him for his knowledge too.

'God sure made you smart; all you need now is Jesus in your heart. Hey that even rhymes praise God', I said as we looked at each other and chuckled while we hugged.

Tina and I eventually went to the spare trailer to get ready to sleep. We first blessed the inside with the holy oil we had brought.

We then sat by the fire a while before retiring, talking with strangers that knew my brother and Babette. At one point Tina noticed one young man who was present holding a beer and wearing a cross around his neck which was hanging upside down. She informed me it was something a Satanist wore.

We had a chance to witness to a young man about Christ who informed us what the Satanist's he knew of in the nearby city practiced. He mentioned he was no longer interested in it mainly because they had sacrificed animals. We could see that his spirit was struggling with what was really important in life and Tina told him about faith in Christ and was an effective humble witness to him.

It was a blessing to be able to share our experiences with him. We believe God used us that night and protected us from some of the insanity of the spirits around us.

We were buffered from the evil around us. Tina noticed two demon spirits standing around outside of our trailer before we went to sleep.

The next morning we had a chance to encourage and pray for one of Babette's nieces who was getting married in a few weeks. She was a humble soul and we had a real soft spot for her telling her we would be praying for her and her husband on their special day.

My brother and Babette were supposed to play a song as she walked down the aisle—they practiced the beautiful melody for her bringing tears of joy to her eyes.

Tina and I believed we were meant to be there even for just the one day. It was edifying for us to witness for Christ and to just be a part of my brother's life for a short while, meeting good people and standing up for Gods will.

As we drove home Tina told me that while I was working at the Park Sets Motel last year, she would sometimes wake up in the middle of the night.

She said as I would be sleeping she noticed I looked extremely pale lying on my back with my arms crossed in front of me. She would notice that this was not normal almost demonic, like I was in a coffin so she would lay her hand on me and pray. Then she would drive to work the next day and feel spirits attached to her and would have to cast them off of her. She wasn't sure why she hadn't told me until now but it was more confirmation to me of the evil that had somehow found its way inside of me even back then.

During the next week I was doing more and more scripture reading and praying. I could still feel like I wasn't totally free of all spirits that were oppressing me. I thought maybe there was at least one more that was trying to hide and torment me so I went back into the washroom another night to the mirror to make sure, and I confronted anything else that might still be there. I commanded the 'nephew of the lord' spirit to come forth in Jesus' name. There was a slight stirring in me as my countenance changed. Another one was gone, leaving me feeling much lighter and more at peace.

I have checked a number of times whether anything else would surface. Nothing did. I brought a lot of infected artifacts home with me. Souvenirs from the old haunted motel. I talked to the ghosts which were really demons, fallen angels. That was a grave decision. That's what really brought the attacks. I opened myself up.

They're evil and try to scare us and don't care about you or me. They will try to kill you off if they want to. I assumed I was safe enough talking to them. I was wrong. That mistake almost cost me my life, more than once. The spirit world has different ways of affecting us humans. We can let them into our space by blatantly sinning or they can be sent to us from evil hearted people, satanists for example with their evil intentions.

Sometimes by praying for other peoples salvation we can provoke attacks. Doing deliverance on an oppressed or possessed person can sometimes bring on demonic attacks or can transfer the evil spirit [s] to the person or people casting the spirit [s] out, similar to a séance which in my opinion is very dangerous. A demon can kill if its allowed to.

This is one more reason why being covered with Christ's blood is vitally important. The ultimate protection against evil is being one of His saved children. Unless a person is born again they cannot enter God's kingdom. That is scriptural truth and spoken by Jesus himself found in holy text, the gospel book of John. [Ch. 3: 3-8].

Acknowledging that I could do nothing to save myself without Christ's saving grace was my first step to real freedom. I had to let God change my heart so that my tendency to sin could be changed a little at a time and supernaturally by God. To sin is always a choice. There are blessings and curses in life.

Praying regularly and learning truth in scripture is important. Being assertive when confronting evil and using the authority I have in Christ's name against the spirit world is also important. I trust the only true God and Saviour of this world, Jesus Christ of Nazareth. Come soon Lord Jesus.

You can know the truth and the truth will set you free. Christ is the truth in everything. He knows what's in your heart.

Remember Him and His saving grace **before** death.

About The Author

Like a lot of people I have learned that the world has many ways to try to acquire peace, wealth and happiness. Over the past thirty years or so I have dabbled in different spiritual schools of thought and adventures, none of which have provided any lasting success in my life, or a feeling of peace and self worth.

In fact any so called organized road I have tried to find lasting truth in has lead to unhappiness and destruction for the most part, like some of you readers can relate to.

A life without Christ is a life wasted, of sadness and futility. Life without salvation is death. The way of truth became more of a reality while renovating the motel.

I have studied and practiced eastern and western astrology, have been a practicing solitary witch, was a Scientologist, grew up Catholic, nearly enrolled as a Jehovah's Witness, and practiced the new age philosophies. I was also into Buddhism and the martial arts and different forms of worldly self defense.

I am a believer in Christ living near Toronto Canada.

My wife Cristina offers Christian prayer counseling including help for victims of satanic ritual abuse.

We have a ministry called Carry The Cross Deliverance Ministries, located in Mississauga, On Canada. This ministry caters to the needs of anyone who is oppressed or possessed by the demonic.

We are independent and are not affiliated with any organization. We try to live our lives for God and serve others as believers. We are part of a team who help clear homes and artifacts of demonic and poltergeist activity. More information to contact us can be found by visiting the website;

www.carrythecrossdeliveranceministries.com

www.ingramcontent.com/pod-product-compliance
Lightning Source LLC
Chambersburg PA
CBHW061637040426
42446CB00010B/1452